S

RINGSIDE SEAT

RINGSIDE SEAT

The Political and Wartime
Memoirs of James Allason

James Allason

TIMEWELL
PRESS

First published in Great Britain by
Timewell Press Limited
10 Porchester Terrace, London W2 3TL

Published by Timewell Press Limited 2007

A catalogue record for this title is available from the
British Library.

ISBN-10: 1-85725-223-3
ISBN-13: 978-1-85725-223-1

Typeset by TW Typesetting, Plymouth, Devon
Manufactured in the EU by L.P.P.S. Ltd, Wellingborough,
Northants NN8 3PJ

Contents

James Allason 1946.

Margaret Thatcher with Denis at Chequers. On the fence – an unfamiliar position for 'the Lady'.

Photo by Srdja Djukanovi

Foreword

The title of this book is not exactly right. Rather than occupying a ringside seat, James Allason has more often than not been at the centre of the action, in a veritable hot seat. Fighting the Japanese, arguing with Mountbatten and Wingate, and serving Churchill in the Cabinet War Rooms, James was rarely just a spectator. In Parliament he knew and observed seven Prime Ministers at close quarters, and shaped critical areas of policy behind the scenes. But for his championship of the right to buy their homes, millions of council house tenants might never have had the opportunity to do so.

Many of decisive episodes in the history of Britain in the twentieth century found James at the centre of the action, as a soldier, military planner, and later as a politician with a singular grasp of the issues that mattered to ordinary people. He has known virtually all of the principal actors on the political stage, and well beyond. Only James could have counselled humility to the Viceroy of India, ordered Enoch Powell's arrest as a suspect Japanese spy, or subjected the Shah of Iran to an interrogation about opium production. In holding Attlee to manageable military objectives in Palestine he inadvertently created the window in which the State of Israel was established.

From this ringside seat we gain unexpected insights into many of the personalities who shaped Britain in the twentieth century, and into complex episodes, such as the Profumo Affair, that have since become encrusted with legend. As ever, the truth is more fascinating than fiction. And, from James's dry pen, much funnier.

Margaret Thatcher

The Rt. Hon. Baroness Thatcher, LG, OM, FRS

1

Beginnings

I was born in September 1912, at my grandfather's house in South Kensington, and family legend has it that I attended the opera the night before, which may account for my lifelong interest in music and the opera.

Four years earlier, my father, Walter, had asked permission from Vice Admiral James Poland to marry his daughter, but when he said he lived on an army captain's pay, he was shown the door. He returned to his mother, a thrifty widow who had inherited several acres of Kensington, and she agreed to grant him an allowance that enabled him to meet Admiral Poland's requirements. The couple were married, and on their honeymoon Walter took time off to win the Plunging Championship of England, an aquatic feat he achieved six times between 1896 and 1926.

Plunging was a popular item in swimming competitions but was abandoned in the 1930s because it took too long. Each competitor was allowed one minute to dive in and see how far he could reach, floating motionless. The world record was eighty-five feet, and my father's best was a few inches short of this. He continued to compete in the army and the inter-service championships until his army retirement at the age of fifty-five, never beaten. As his bulk increased so did his proficiency. It was dramatic to see him break the surface half-way down the pool like a whale, travelling fast.

The couple were blissfully happy for five years, but in 1913 my mother was carrying her baby upstairs when she tripped at the top of the stairs and fell headlong, ensuring only that she protected me. She was found dead at the foot of the stairs and I was saved. My father never really got over his loss and when war came the following year he threw himself into combat, fighting in the front-line for the entire period of the conflict. He enjoyed patrolling at night in no man's land, even as a battalion commander. I am reminded of General Jack Seeley, who in his memoirs wrote, 'My batman should have had the VC, for he followed me everywhere'. Walter commanded a company at the battle of Mons, and thereafter found relief in killing Germans. Apart from when he was recovering from his wounds, he remained at the front continuously, and was decorated twice with the Distinguished Service Order. (His exploits, drawn from diaries, are recorded in *Annals of the Allason Family*).

Meanwhile, from infancy I was left to be brought up by an embittered maiden aunt and a succession of nannies. Her beautiful sister had married into the Soames family and when her husband was killed she kept open house for Allied officers, especially Russians. Meanwhile, her less attractive sister had to look after her mother and an annoying nephew while all the eligible men were getting killed. In 1917, as a four-year-old, I was asleep in my cot with four high brass rails when a bomb dropped by a Zeppelin detonated close by. There was a large painting above my cot, and it fell, neatly forming a lid, which protected me from the wall that collapsed on top of it. We spent the rest of the night under the billiard table in case the roof fell in.

My grandfather, the admiral, walked over the next day to see how we were, but when he saw the damaged and deserted house, he suffered a heart attack from which he died. His brother, Sir Harry Poland, QC, lived on to the age of ninety-nine.

Sir Harry, whose autobiography he modestly entitled 'Seventy-two Years at the Bar', was notoriously badly dressed, so my grandmother sent him to Poole's, then the best tailor in London. The result was as bad as ever, so my grandmother summoned Poole for an explanation. 'He said he spent most of his life sitting down, and insisted upon being measured seated.' I recall Sir Harry wearing a black jacket with striped trousers, a white starched shirt and black bow tie.

Great-uncle Harry recalled for us an occasion when he was on his way to collect an umbrella from the repairers. It was raining so he had to take another brolly. On the omnibus he mistakenly picked up the umbrella of the lady sitting next to him instead of his own, and apologised. On the return journey he encountered the same lady. Observing him with two umbrellas, she remarked, 'I see you have had a successful day.'

Daily Graphic   19th August 1908

THE CAR AND THE HONEYMOON

The marriage of Captain W. Allanson and Miss K. M. Poland at St. Peter's, Cranley Gardens, yesterday, provided an unusual feature for those outside the church after the ceremony.   Captain and

The bride and bridegroom start for their honeymoon.

Mrs. Allanson left at once for their honeymoon in Captain Allanson's motor-car, which was waiting outside, and Captain Allanson himself started the car and acted as his own chauffeur.

Report of the marriage of James's parents in August 1908. The reporter was so shocked by Walter driving himself away that he misspelled the family name.

Chacombe Priory near Banbury afforded James four days hunting a week on visits home.

Photo by Jamie Allason

My ten year old 3 litre Bentley in 1935. I had replaced the standard vertical windscreen with a fold-flat screen of my own design.

Guard mounting at the Viceroy's House, New Delhi. The building on the left housed the Government Secretariat, that on the right was GHQ India, where I worked.'

When the admiral visited King Rama V of Siam he politely enquired how many children the monarch had. The king did not know, but sent for his chief wife to inquire. The answer was seventy-two, thus far.

My grandmother's next house in London had a back extension with a lavatory on the ground floor. Aged six, I was on its roof while my older sister, Dolores, known as Lola, was in the garden below. She told me to stand on the skylight, which I obediently did. She then instructed me to jump up and down. As a result I descended in a shower of glass upon my aunt, who was seated upon the throne below. It seemed to me unfair that it was I who was punished.

About this time, my father drove at night into a traffic island in Regent Street. He took a taxi home, and got the driver to help him up two flights of stairs. He went to bed without disturbing anyone. In the morning he was found to have broken his leg in two places. I saw him rarely, for he did not come to take charge of me until 1922, after returning from service during the Troubles in Ireland.

A cousin, Jack Holmes, was captain of Sussex's cricket team, and he insisted I should go to the county ground at Hove for coaching by such legends as Maurice Tate and A.E.R. Gilligan. Unfortunately, they weaned me off my cow shot, which scored boundaries, and having been taught a straight bat I never scored another run.

When my uncle, Harry, was at Harrow with Winston Churchill, the school ethic had been, 'It's swagger to swot', so neither of them sought, or achieved, any academic success. Accordingly I was sent elsewhere. Haileybury, near Hertford, had been founded by the East India Company as a college to train its cadets, and became a public school only in the mid-nineteenth century. Its houses were named after distinguished old boys, such as Lawrence of the Punjab. The last thus named was Allenby, so Attlee had to go without a house to his name.

After attending a prep school where everyone was friendly, entering public school came as a nasty shock. Boys were regarded as being in urgent need of discipline, to be enforced by liberal application of physical punishment. Perhaps one in ten of the masters showed signs of being possessed of humanity. Moreover Haileybury was set in deep Hertfordshire countryside with no urban amenities nearby, such as public houses, sweet shops or cinemas, so there were few distractions from games.

Despite initial trepidation, I soon made friends. My contemporaries, Cuthbert Alport, Geoffrey de Freitas and Chris Mayhew, entered the

Commons after the war, but Alport had risen to the Lords before I arrived at Westminister. Another contemporary was Peter Townsend, amiable and good-looking, a view with which Princess Margaret would come to agree.

The new boys in my house thought the head boy insufferably arrogant, so I arranged mass prayers in our dormitory for him to be removed through some mishap. It was therefore highly embarrassing when he contracted polio.

In the Easter school holidays of 1926 my father took me, aged thirteen, on my first visit overseas, to Malta, there to visit our lifelong friends, the Worralls. This was exciting, and an opportunity to get to know my father better – and for him to understand me. He and Colonel Worrall had met in the Great War, and when our families encountered each other at Aldershot in 1923 we became great friends. In the 1930s they inherited a country house in Warwickshire not ten miles from ours. Claude was the only one of six children to marry, but he had six children. Having commanded 3rd Coldstream, he was shocked when his three daughters all married Welsh Guardsmen. One, Charles, became Chief of the Defence Staff, Lord Guthrie. On our 1926 visit, travelling by train, we woke up in Switzerland, and I had my first view of the gorgeous Alps. It was to prove an inspiration. We stopped in Rome and Naples to enjoy the sights before catching a boat from Syracuse to Malta. Travelling with my father proved to be anything but dull: as in war, adventure pursued him.

We enjoyed a picnic at St Pauls Bay, but were besieged by beggars. Colonel Worrall, always a stickler for discipline, lined them up, tallest on the right, shortest on the left, before distributing the leftovers.

On our way back we stopped in Paris and visited the Folies-Bergère, where Josephine Baker was appearing for the first time, then dressed in a ring of bananas and nothing else. It was an encouraging experience for a thirteen-year-old. Sir Harry Poland did not approve of the visit, so when his sister, Aunt Emily, consulted him about her will, her bequest was made directly to me instead of through my father. Thus, at sixteen, I inherited £3,000 absolutely (now equivalent to £100,000), which has been very helpful to fall back on.

Because of my poor eyesight I was hopeless at games at Haileybury, but the fact that I was the school's best mathematician drew no applause. I did not attract any of the bullies after I discovered that if you vigorously attacked a bully and hurt him, he would be inclined to go after easier targets thereafter. In any event I had now hit six foot in height. It was compulsory to watch cricket matches, and nothing was allowed to interfere with attendance. So I kept a running estimate of when the innings should end, judging by the scoreboard and my watch. The teaching was unimaginative, except our enjoyable German lessons, which consisted of singing songs and learning verse.

Rex Whistler had been in my house until a year or two before I arrived, and there were drawings of his remaining there. I was astonished at his craftsmanship. I mourn the loss of Rupert Brooke in the First World War, and of Whistler in the second. What further joy they might have brought!

The art master at Haileybury was Wilfred Blunt, elder brother of the future Sir Anthony Blunt, art historian, MI5 officer and traitor. It was Wilfred who encouraged what became a lifelong interest in painting. My study was decorated with reproductions of Degas pastels, long before the impressionists became popular. Blunt later moved to Eton, where he taught John Merton, and in his retirement became curator of the Watts Museum near Guildford. When I paid a visit to the gallery I called on Blunt, who was kind enough to pretend to remember me. I mentioned that when I had been his pupil he had been copying an El Greco in the National Gallery; he then beckoned me into his dining room where it hung. He told me that the National Gallery's director had been dining with him recently and had kept looking at the El Greco. Blunt had said to him, 'You are thinking, "that old fool believes he has an El Greco, but it isn't one". I know, because I painted it myself.'

I spent the last eighteen months of school in the maths sixth form, where the boy who came second to me won an exhibition to Oxford, but I was due for the army exam. I did appallingly badly in the two maths papers, as they were on topics I had long forgotten, but I received top marks for history, which I had not been taught recently. I would have passed second into Sandhurst, but instead was nineteenth at the Royal Military Academy, Woolwich, then the military Winchester to Sandhurst's Eton.

In 1926, after giving up command of his regiment, my father and Colonel Henry Wilson were appointed joint chief umpires for the great Aldershot manoeuvres, in those days the army's largest scale training event. These two heavyweights galloping across Laffans Plain became known as "the two jumbos". Wilson's nickname stuck with him all the way to becoming a field marshal and Supreme Allied Commander in the Mediterranean in the Second World War.

The commander-in-chief at Aldershot was General Sir Philip Chetwode, a splendid figure nicknamed Bart on account of his baronetcy and patrician manner. He was none the less a serious soldier who, with Allenby, had taken Jerusalem in 1917. A close friend of T. E. Lawrence, he would later be responsible for getting him to enlist in the Royal Tank Corps under the pseudonym T. E. Shaw. In 1926 he was appointed commander-in-chief of the army in India. He gave us his labrador, Bella, who became a great companion. Bella had been schooled at Sandringham shoots. On one of the drives there most of the birds streamed over a single gun. The gun to the right decided to tease his friend who had drawn the favoured spot by poaching birds flying across his front and dropping them at his pal's feet. At the end of the drive he found that King George V had replaced his friend, and like his grandmother, the king was not amused.

Later, when Chetwode's daughter Penelope became engaged to John Betjeman, Bart said to him, 'I've been considering how you should address me. Philip is too informal, and Lord Chetwode too distant, so I think you'd better just call me Field Marshal'.

The following year my father was given his last appointment, commanding a territorial infantry brigade in Scotland. He took a furnished house in Ayrshire to which my sister, Lola, and I duly followed him. It had two long drives leading to the front steps. One day Elizabeth, the parlour-maid, saw an old lady walking up one of the drives, so she went and opened the front door, to find nobody there. We did not tell Elizabeth that the ghost of a former resident was said to call.

Apart from the ghost, the house was always alive with guests, and one frequent visitor was Lord Glasgow, who walked the eight miles from the coast across his moors to play tennis with us, and then walked home to Kelburn Castle. We hunted with the Eglington, where the master was the renowned Jack Coates, and with the Lanark & Renfrew, whose master was Lord Inverclyde. Marrying a saucy actress named June Tripp, whose stage name was simply 'June', he was embarrassed when the London Midland and Scottish Railway advertised a local beauty spot with the slogan, 'Come and see Inverclyde in June'.

I stayed with Jack Mann-Thompson in the Highlands, and it was his boast that he had sailed his yacht into Kiel harbour in the summer of 1914 flying the white ensign as a member of the Royal Yacht Squadron. The Kaiser, a fellow member, signalled that he would come aboard, so Jack had promptly sailed out. Even to my sixteen year old self this seemed poor manners, so I was not surprised when I heard Mann-Thompson say to his butler, 'This wine is corked. Give it to the ladies.' Said to be the richest man in Ayrshire, he was proud that it was his grandfather who had made the family fortune, when so many of his wealthy contemporaries were obliged to their fathers. These he considered *nouveaux riches*.

In those days we walked the long distance from one butt or hide on a grouse moor to the next. Between butts we found a spring in the heather, and all had a drink. I was impressed by one guest, who said, 'This fluid is extremely pleasant. I must try it again some time.'

At the other end of the entertainment spectrum was the music hall tradition, still thriving in the pantomimes Lola and I enjoyed visiting. At the Glasgow Empire a noted comedian called Tommy Lorne played the dame in Cinderella. In one scene as the dame was preparing for the ball Buttons said, 'Then we must have charlotte russe'. 'Charlotte Russe? She's not coming here.' To which the retort was, 'But charlotte russe is a tart.' The rejoinder to that was, 'And that's why she's not coming.'

Our neighbours in Ayrshire seemed no less eccentric. Mrs Hay-Boyd used to attend the Western meetings at Ayr races, wearing a different-coloured dress and flamboyant hat each day. She was invariably accompanied by her mad son, George, and his keeper. One day the latter complained he no longer enjoyed smoking, only to hear George explain that he had found his smoking annoying, but had seen an advertisement to cure smoking called 'Tasteless in tea'. 'I got it for you,' he revealed, proving he was not all that mad after all.

After this happy Scottish interlude I began to prepare for Woolwich where I had heard that my cousin Philip Mead had established his reputation there by greasing the tramlines on Shooters Hill, just outside the main gate, so the trams were unable to gain a grip, and gradually they all accumulated at the foot of the hill. Not long afterwards there had been a riot on the train after the annual Woolwich-Sandhurst rugger match. This had resulted in Questions in the Commons. We were accordingly warned to behave ourselves. Few heeded the advice, especially as there was a tradition of mischief from the seniors when they passed out of the acadamy. When the next most senior course to mine was due to pass out, all our chamberpots were commandeered by the senior cadets and placed on the roof parapet to provide a decoration for the parade.

Outraged by this inconvenience, I climbed on to the roof with a friend late that night and moved the pots out of sight. However, the next day, when the short-sighted General Dobbie came to take the salute he remarked on the 'unusual decorations', having been tipped off by his son. The seniors, with their backs to the building, laughed at his joke, while we intermediates laughed at the seniors. The juniors, known as snookers, were merely puzzled.

The adjutant, Captain Brian Kimmins, appeared to be very fierce, but he was probably over-compensating for his brother Anthony, whose play, *While Parents Sleep*, was raising eyebrows in the West End. I was to meet him again in more trying circumstances.

In our senior term a night guard was introduced to give all the cadets experience of night-time sentry duty. One evening, as a joke, we delivered a cadet to the guard to be put into the guardroom for being drunk, but were repelled by buckets of water. The authorities misinterpreted our prank as a protest against mounting the guard. Later we were able to dispel this impression at the end-of-term concert when we demonstrated we could joke about guard mounting to a tune from Faust. 'I have come to turn out the guard.' 'Sir, you must not turn out the guard because it has been turned out once already and twice would be too hard.'

My contribution to the concert concerned an instructor who owned an old crock of a car. A cardboard cut-out of it appeared on the stage, and was stolen while I, as his impersonation, sang, to a tune from *White House Inn*:

> 'She goes, she goes,
> Beneath my very nose
> She goes and where
> She's going to Lord knows.'

I was unfortunately unaware that his wife had just run away, but was agreeable when the car's gender was changed to 'it' by the tactful censor.

The Riding School at Woolwich was tough, and we were required to vault on and off the horse at a canter. Although I had ridden for years, I was invariably subjected to strong criticism, while Mr Dawson, a less experienced rider, always received praise. When I was selected to ride in the competition against Sandhurst, I asked why not Mr Dawson, and was told, 'He needed encouragement, you didn't.'

When entering the army exam, I had applied for Woolwich above Sandhurst because it was more difficult. At Woolwich I had put in for Sappers (Royal Engineers) before Gunners (Royal Artillery) for the same reason. Towards the end of the Woolwich course, I attended a lecture for intending Sapper officers, and asked about the prospects of riding. The answer came that there was little horseback riding in the Sappers. I suppose I could have applied to change my priorities, but instead did deliberately badly in the final exams, and so just missed the last Sapper place.

2

The Army Pre-War

My first posting was to a gunner battery at Fareham and army life began in earnest. I learned that as an officer I was entitled to a charger, a groom and sufficient forage for two mounts, so I put this privilege to best use by buying two polo ponies and a point-to-pointer to race. The charger turned out to be quite a good hunter, so for the next few years there were two horses out to grass winter and summer, and two in action. I played polo at the naval ground at Gosport and hunted with the Hambledon.

My father had now returned home to Chacombe Priory, near Banbury. At the start of two months' leave I brought my two hunters down, and was kept busy hunting two days a week with the Bicester, two with the Grafton, shooting one day, and spending another in London. Chacombe was rambling, somewhat tumbledown and not notably warm. This was unsurprising since its origins, and some of the plumbing arrangements, appeared to date back to medieval times; not that this stopped us skating on the lake when it froze over in winter.

For the rest of the year we skated on Sundays at a private club which met at the Oxford ice-rink. My statuesque sister, Lola, was waltzing on the ice with the diminutive Lord Sandford, when someone remarked, 'Does not that resemble a battleship with a tug?' 'Not at all,' replied Archie Southby, then Solicitor-General. 'Battleships have flat bottoms.' Another enthusiastic skater, Lord Redesdale, brought his younger daughters, the Mitford sisters. Unity, who was to become a favourite of Hitler, always looked grumpy, while Deborah, the future Duchess of Devonshire, was but a schoolgirl; Pam, however, became a close friend. She married an eccentric millionaire Oxford don, Derek Jackson, who had previously been married to Augustus John's daughter, Poppet.

Derek Jackson was said to be one of the five men in the world who could talk mathematics to Albert Einstein. He also rode regularly in the Grand National, usually falling after several fences. He and his twin brother owned the *News of the World*. Once, when I reproached him, he said it was a good Tory paper. I replied that no one bought the *News of the World* to read the editorial.

Knowing my interest in advanced mathematics, Derek advised me to read *Wave Mechanics* by Alan Turing, then an undergraduate at King's College, Cambridge, and just three months older than myself. Thus I became one of the first outside the confines of academia to encounter the work of the genius who was to play a decisive role in developing the computers used by the cryptographers at Bletchley Park that would help shorten the Second World War. In 1939 he would be the first mathematician to be recruited by the government for secret work, and his interest in quantum mechanics and logical mathematics proved invaluable to the codebreakers who needed machines to assist their calculations, especially when they were attempting to test millions of permutations, too many to be undertaken in the very limited time available under wartime conditions.

When war came Jackson's work involved solving mathematical problems for the government so secret that he was not permitted to know what they were about. Fed up with this, he joined the RAF and flew regularly as a rear gunner in bombers over Germany until the authorities discovered how one of the best brains in Britain was being employed. He was immediately grounded, but used his airborne experience to invent 'Window', the thin strips of metal foil which, when dropped from Allied aircraft, mimicked the returns received by German radar, thus neutralising the enemy's ability to predict air-raids. He also saved many Allied lives by his discovery of the purpose of an apparently innocuous electronic gadget recovered from a downed Ju-88 bomber. He suspected the equipment homed in on the rear-looking 'Monica' radar fitted to all Bomber Command aircraft to detect enemy night-fighters; tests at Farnborough proved him correct. The 'Flensburg' device could home in on a British bomber from a range of 130 miles, and once he had explained this to Air Chief Marshal Harris, 'Monica' was withdrawn immediately, with a considerable net saving of life.

After the war Derek and Pam moved to Ireland, where he abandoned her and went to France to work as a nuclear physicist, marrying three more wives.

The winter of 1933–34 was the first time that I had a full season's hunting available, so I decided to try skiing in February, when my horses would be glad of a rest and frost was likely to cancel hunting. On this, my first skiing holiday, I was determined not to join a ski class. I found that the favoured Christiana or Christie turn was very similar to stopping on ice-skates, so I was soon able to ski fast, and became committed to the sport for life, if never its most elegant exponent.

In 1935 I went with some friends to Innsbruck, but the conditions were dreadful. There was no snow below the half station of the funicular, and the second section ascended to the summit of the mountain. Patsy Richardson, a skiing friend of the doyen of British skiers, Bill Bracken, took me to the top. The descent was said to be the steepest in the Alps, and was icy with rocks showing, but somehow I managed to get down, shaken but without a fall. On the second day I decided to leave my friends and move to Davos. There I found the best skiing in Europe and would regularly return for the next sixty-five years.

Back home I bought a three-litre Bentley in the summer of 1933 and, after replacing the standard windscreen with a fold-flat screen of my own design, took up motor sport. My friend Peter Reed, with whom I became a founder member of the Vintage Sports Car Club, went rather further with the purchase of an ex-team Le Mans Aston Martin, and an ex Malcolm Campbell Bugatti. Peter preferred to drive on the right-hand side of the road, swerving to the left only to let an oncoming car go by. He could thus drive at about twice the speed of the traffic on his left. There were no centre white lines in those days, and few cars.

Peter fell in love with a rather plain girl in Lee-on-Solent, but the passion was unrequited. Forlorn and sleepless he regularly drove his Bugatti to London, round Piccadilly Circus, back to Gosport, then completed a second round trip. One morning after dawn on his second return journey he rounded a corner at about ninety m.p.h. and encountered a flock of sheep blocking the road. He contrived to stop just short of the flock, but the police measured his skid marks at ninety-two yards. This puzzled the magistrates, Peter being vague as to his speed. So they asked him how fast his car could go. He was reluctant to say 120 m.p.h. but when asked if the car could do as much as sixty m.p.h. he had to admit to that. 'A very bad case: fined £20 and licence suspended for six months' was the verdict. So I had to sneak the Bugatti away from the court. Foolishly, he had driven it there. Had the magistrates seen the sleek blue racer they would surely have doubled the penalty.

One of the cars I drove was the 1907 fourteen-and-a-half-litre Grand Prix Itala, which is now in the National Motor Museum at Beaulieu. Weighing just over a ton, it had a top speed of 100 m.p.h. but flimsy brakes, so the best means of decelerating was to change down, a course not available at high speed.

The 1920s had seen the introduction of front-wheel brakes, and high-performance sports cars become more manageable. A friend owned Tim Birkin's supercharged four-and-a-half litre four-seater Bentley, in which Birkin won the Pau Grand Prix, to the horror of the French, who objected to such a *camion* being entered. Another pal had an eight-litre two-seater Bentley, but would not exceed 140 m.p.h. because he could not trust the tyres. Unfortunately it was the firm of Bentley which went bust in the financial crisis of 1931, but its products remained highly prized by a younger generation, me included.

I spent many summer Saturdays at Brooklands, the first British motor racing circuit. Two steeply banked concrete curves, thirty feet high, were joined by straights, providing a three-and-a-quarter-mile outer circuit, for high-speed racing. There was also the mountain circuit which included a terrifying hairpin bend. Events varied from racing car days and those for sports cars. It was thrilling to watch the racing cars but even better to participate in the sports car races.

These interests kept me fully occupied at a time when many friends were at university, and I recall meeting an officer from another unit who had just come down from Cambridge, where he had read medieval French history. I asked the subject of his thesis, and he replied, 'Someone you would not have heard of, Anne de Montmorency, Constable of France.' By some satisfying chance I was able to reply, 'Did you not know that he pronounced his name Ann-ay?'

According to gunner custom, everyone had to move on to a new posting every three years. So in the autumn of 1936 I was sent to the Boys' Battery at the Royal Artillery Depot at Woolwich, where my duties appeared to be limited to watching while boy soldiers were taught the trumpet by NCOs. This allowed me plenty of time to spend the season hunting from home, so I probably slept more nights at

Chacombe than at Woolwich that winter. The boys had normal school holidays, so my leave had to be taken then, which meant two ski trips, at the New Year and Easter. This was before the development of mechanical ski-lifts, and as Scheidegg, in Switzerland, was the best place for spring skiing, the experts tended to congregate there.

During the Easter holiday of 1937 I found myself on the mountain railway sitting opposite a pretty American blonde; on arrival at Scheidegg she was greeted by her husband, Count Haugwitz-Reventlow. She was, I learned, Barbara Hutton, the Woolworth heiress, and he was captain of the Danish national ski team, which she sponsored. There was still time for one run down the slopes that afternoon, so I caught another train up. Two other passengers also got out, and they led me to the edge of the Punch Bowl. The first took it straight, his voice floating back, 'It's bloody fast.' The second man put in two Christie turns before taking the rest of the descent straight. I put in four Christies, and when I reached the others I found that they were Chris Mackintosh, perhaps the greatest British skier ever, and Lord Beaverbrook's son, Max Aitken, whom Chris was coaching as a candidate for the British team.

That evening I asked Bill Bracken if I could join his racing class and he told me to come out the next day and follow immediately behind him. We went fast down a steep glade, when Bracken suddenly checked with a broad stem and then crashed to a halt at the side. Being just behind him, I was able to do the same, but the rest of the class were falling about with cries of 'Blast you Bill', so I was allowed to join. Bracken was slim, of medium height, with broad shoulders. On the slopes he dressed in dark tight Vorlage skiing trousers, a double-breasted jacket of bright red, with a cap, the tail of which trailed between his shoulder blades. He skied with his feet always together, with his arms outstretched, skimming the slopes with the grace of a ballet dancer. In contrast, Chris Mackintosh was like a giant hurtling down the mountain. One evening Mackintosh and I were in the Scheidegg bar, when Katie, the beautiful wife of Ziggy Dyson-Taylor, rushed in with tears and mascara pouring down her face, shouting, 'Help, help, Ziggy is beating me.' Chris observed that it was time Ziggy went to sleep and felled him with a single blow. We carried him to bed, and he woke the next morning in a pool of blood. Ziggy was an excellent skier, but was too fond of the bottle to make the British team.

In the Bracken class were Jimmy Gardiner and Peter Aitchison, both members of the British team, D'Egville the cartoonist, and John Johannides, a former member of the British team who skied in grey flannel trousers to emphasise the fact that he never fell. Bill's wife, Babs, wore an elegant skirt, perhaps for the same reason, but I took her photograph on the only occasion she fell that year. The hotel at Scheidegg was like a huge house party as it was the only one there, and among the other friends I made that season were the actor John Mills, and Louis Chiron, the racing driver.

Bill Bracken was then concentrating on teaching a new technique he had invented, known as the 'Parallel Swing', in which the skis were kept firmly together. To turn, you put your weight as far forward as possible, pressed down, then up, which unweighted the backs of your skis and round you went. This required your heels clamped firmly to the ski, a problem then solved by the steel cable of the Kandahar binding, albeit somewhat to the detriment of safety.

When my parents had skied at St Moritz before the Great War, she in a long skirt, leather bindings allowed the heel to rise, giving little control of the ski. The V-shaped stem was possible, but the best turn was the Telemark, where you slid one ski forward and went down with the knee on to the other, locking the ski tip of one to your boot on the other leg. A slight edge to the leading ski propelled one round without further effort. My father once led a friend and his two children up the Celerina Valley to Corviglia with St Moritz spread out below them. The friend said, 'Children, this is very dangerous; take your skis off and we will walk down.' So my father had to ski down alone. Actually, he preferred the Cresta toboggan run to skiing, and in those days the sledge riders wore no protection. During one descent his leg went over the edge at the Battledore curve, and ice cut it to the bone, but it was so cold that he did not notice. When he got to the bottom he observed a lot of blood and commented that someone had had a nasty accident. 'Yes,' they said, 'It's you.' He spent the next two months in hospital.

The first step towards holding down the heel was the Amstutz spring, attaching the ankle to the back of the ski, although it still allowed the heel to rise somewhat. In about 1935, however, the Kandahar cable binding became almost universally used, at the expense of many broken ankles and torn Achilles tendons. In 1937 I bought a pair of French 'Superdiagonal' rubber straps, which fitted over the ankle and clipped to the ski behind the heel. On a forward fall, the clip gave way, and the heel was released. I once gave myself two black eyes on the tips of my skis, which at least proved that I had my skis well together.

One day, Arnold Lunn, the grand old man of British skiing and inventor of the slalom race, jeered at the Bracken class that they could not do a Telemark. I promptly unclipped my straps and demonstrated one. When I sought a replacement for my 'Superdiagonals' after the war, I found that the French firm had sold out to the Swiss binding manufacturers, who then suppressed the revolutionary system. It was not until about 1955 that toe release bindings were invented and damage to the ankle was transferred to the knee.

I have skied with most of the best English women skiers of my day, including Nell Carroll, Audrey Sale-Barker, Soss Roe and Hilary Laing, but never with Evie Pinchin, a neighbour and friend. Evie was then a tall and willowy blonde, very attractive, but in no way muscular like the others. She took part in the 1938 World Ski Championship at Innsbruck, but there was a heavy thaw followed by a sharp frost so the downhill course was extremely dangerous, with the final sector being an icy path through uncovered tree stumps. The bravest woman won, and that was Evie.

After the war, and completely unfit, Evie went to Chamonix to start again and the town was flattered to receive the still reigning world champion and gave her a smart young ski guide. He took her down one slope that required a sharp left turn with a safety net to prevent skiers from falling into the valley, but her guide simply jumped the net. Evie later told me she had about three seconds to choose between British honour and life and limb, so she jumped the net and survived.

Before the Second World War there were only about a dozen ski-lifts and very few pistes, and those that existed on popular runs, such as Weissfluh-Klosters, were quite narrow from lack of use, so we skied in all kinds of snow with Bracken showing that the parallel swing worked in every snow condition except breakable crust. Later, in India, two Telemark enthusiasts said that they heard that the parallel swing worked in soft snow; would I care to demonstrate? They set off in deep soft snow in graceful Telemark curves, while I had to work very hard lifting the backs of my skis, so that I arrived panting.

When the summer of 1937 came, I played polo on Ham Common, and did some motor racing with my current Bentley, which was now a four-and-a-half litre two-seater. This was the car in which I won sports car races at Brooklands and Donnington. Naturally, I also had my military duties, but they were not very onerous. At King George VI's coronation that year I was assigned the task of taking eighty cadets from all over England to a stand outside Buckingham Palace. They had been selected because they were considered the best in their units, and were therefore very well behaved. After watching the procession leaving the Palace for the Abbey, I strolled over to the Cavalry Club for lunch and came back in time for the return procession to find all was well. The day passed off faultlessly, but I was a little disappointed not to receive a Coronation Medal, the Cavalry Club apparently not being considered to be part of the parade.

In the summer of 1937, my sister and I decided to give a cocktail party in London, so we hired a room in Park Lane and brought Jones the butler up from the country. A late arrival was greeted by a very drunk Jones saying, 'They've gorn to the Calvary Club; they've all gorn to the Calvary Club.' Jones had a fondness for gin. After the war we found all the gin bottles in the cellar to be full of water.

Although based at the depot at Woolwich, I found attending the West End theatre was preferable to dining in the vast Woolwich mess, where I knew no one. *French without Tears* had received poor notices, but I went because an old school friend, Robert Fleming, was in the cast. The audience roared with laughter and afterwards I went backstage to see Fleming, who introduced me to the cast and author, Terence Rattigan. I told him that the critics had been very unfair, and the show should last at least six months. It actually ran for 1,039 performances and was the first of an alternating sequence of comedies and dramas that would establish him as one of the leading playwrights of the era. A slender, elegant figure, still only twenty-five, Rattigan was then prone to a shyness that belied his later persona. His cast were completely unknown, but astutely chosen; they included Rex Harrison, whom I would come to know later, Kay Hammond, Roland Culver and Jessica Tandy.

During that summer the Russian Ballet came to Covent Garden bringing the best dancers in the world, among them Massine, Baronova, Toumanova, Riabouchinska, Lichine and Danilova. Ballet was not yet popular, so I had no difficulty getting a seat and went night after night. As with the opera, my interest in the ballet was to remain with me thereafter.

I recall reading Evelyn Waugh's short story, *Winner Takes All*, in which a favourite son went to Eton and Oxford while his younger brother attended a minor public school and then studied engineering in Birmingham, where he lodged with a working-class family. When his mother discovered he was falling in love with his host's daughter, he was despatched to Australia. Two years later he returned to England with a fiancée whose father owned a million sheep, but his mother promptly resurrected the Birmingham girl, made him do the decent thing by her, while his brother married the heiress.

Something similar happened to a family living nearby. There was a dominant mother, Molly, whose eldest son, Desmond, went to Eton, Oxford and joined the Brigade of Guards, while his brother Ivo went to a lesser school and then into the City. There reality diverged from fiction. Desmond married a worthy girl and ended as a lieutenant-colonel, while Ivo made a fortune at Lloyd's and married a beautiful society girl.

A friend with the surname of Bill was in a nightclub near Salisbury run by Mrs Fox-Pitt, when it was raided by the police. When asked his name and replying Bill, they demanded his full name, John Bill. They moved to the next table and got the reply 'John'. 'Enough of this foolery; what is your proper name?' 'Augustus John.'

Police raids on illegal drinking in clubs were an occupational hazard, except at the 43 Club in London, where Mrs Meyrick kept the local police sergeant sweet for several years, until found out.

For the long summer break, my father, always a motoring enthusiast, arranged a tour to Hungary in his 1928 Fiat saloon, known as the 'Flying Greenhouse'. On arrival in Hungary, we were allotted a splendidly uniformed ADC, Captain Sibrik, to look after the British general and his family. His immediately previous charge had been Hermann Göring, so my father's eccentricities attracted little surprise, and I determined to fulfil his expectations of English gentlemen. We were invited to shoot, and therefore needed to borrow guns. I said that I always shot partridge with a .38 revolver, so one was immediately produced. When I explained that I had been joking, Sibrik, who had readily adjusted to Göring's thigh-slapping 'jokes' about shootings, confessed that he found English humour very peculiar. Near the Rumanian border we participated in a tremendous partridge shoot, accounting for a gigantic bag.

When we reached the capital we stayed on Margaret Island, between Buda and Pest, where there was a nightclub with a revolving glass dance floor. The evening we were there the cabaret was so exotic that another of the guests, the famously unimpressionable Sam Goldwyn, demanded an encore. In those years Hollywood was largely run by Hungarians, while Budapest's nightlife was easily the equal of Berlin's, though marginally less depraved. The master of ceremonies at the notorious Podium cabaret at the Kavehaus Gresham opposite the chain bridge also had a day job working for our Secret Intelligence Service. His assertion that it was the perfect cover was belied by the fact that everyone in Pest seemed to be in on the 'secret'. The station was said to run the biggest expense account in the service, much of it spent at the Gresham, though to what effect remained uncertain. A succession of deputy directors sent out to investigate were treated to such a memorable time and so many sightings of suspicious characters that their reports were invariably favourable, although much of the intelligence transmitted back by the disapproving 'passport officer' at the embassy was judged improbable. But then Budapest genuinely was a hotbed of intrigue, its links back to the Austro-Hungarian empire and to the emerging Third Reich making it a focal point of espionage and arms trading, thus impossible for any intelligence service to ignore.

One of the chief subjects of professional interest was the carousel of visiting VIPs, of whom we represented the lowest echelon. Conveniently for the shadow army of watchers, these tended to congregate at Restaurant Gundel, after forty years safely established as the greatest restaurant in Central Europe. To the serenade of a gypsy string orchestra, whose composition was reputed to alter following police dragnets, the great and the bad dined beneath paintings by Hungarian masters. Károly Gundel had pioneered a lighter, less coronary-inductive school of cooking, though retaining the classic dishes of goose liver and venison. Gundel palacsinta was and continues to be served throughout Hungary, the pancake's filling enriched with rum, raisin, lemon rind and walnuts, and finished with a chocolate sauce. Invariably it is flambéed; but it was not here, for as the headwaiter dryly observed, 'Fire has never been in the recipe. Károly finishes his pancakes in a high oven.'

Firing was, however, very much on the menu just up the road at 60 Andrassy Boulevard, headquarters of the secret police, and possessed of a courtyard for military executions and a basement equipped with torture chambers and a gallows for civilians. In 1945 it would transform itself seamlessly into the HQ of the communist secret police, with a change of uniform but no great alteration in personnel. Even at the time of our visit the driver and escort would speed past, eyes averted, although presumably reports of our movements were being filed by the bemused Captain Sibrik.

Later we stayed on the estate of a Hungarian countess who had just imported a pack of English foxhounds, and had then to acquire a Briton to teach her English hound language. The similarities of aristocratic and political life to Anthony Hope's novel *Prisoner of Zenda* were too marked to have been coincidental, and it was certainly the only time in my military career that I saw swords and side-arms worn simultaneously with dress uniform. It was not unknown for both to be deployed in the duels still fought by young officers, sometimes at the slightest provocation.

The tour's surprises were not confined to Hungary, as the failure of the gearbox upon arrival in Czechoslovakia demonstrated. My father had been faithful to Fiat cars since his 1908 tourer, which he had replaced with a 1922 open tourer before the Flying Greenhouse. Fortunately we were at Brno, probably the only place in Europe where aluminium could be welded, so we continued to Prague while the repairs were completed. Reunited with the Flying Greenhouse, we drove through the Sudetenland towards Dresden and Berlin. With Hitler stirring up Germans even beyond his country's frontiers the atmosphere was tense. The largely German population of this border region were in increasing conflict with the Czech central government. Posters abounded advertising meetings to be addressed by the Nazi demagogue Konrad Heinlen, whose largely specious claims of mistreatment of the Sudeten Germans were being orchestrated from Berlin. It was clear that trouble was not far off, and I was therefore dismayed, though not surprised, by the ceding of the Sudetenland to Germany at the Munich agreement of September 1938. The Nazi occupation that swiftly followed triggered the flight and forcible expulsion of the Czech population to the rump of Czechoslovakia, itself to fall victim to German invasion and annexation in March 1939.

We paused briefly in Berlin, where a manic atmosphere prevailed. Schooled in army life, and familiar with German culture, I was none the less shocked to see the grip that the Nazi government now exerted upon everyday life and public acceptance of it. Militant nationalism was in the air. What remained unclear was the extent of the Werhmacht's loyalty to the Party. Certainly the latter were taking no chances and parallel formations such as the SS were already making their presence felt. My father, whose German was fluent and well understood relations between politicians and the high command, saw everything clearly. 'They will all follow orders', he observed presciently. We drove back to England in sombre mood, his thoughts called back upon memories of the Great War and the comrades lost, though, as usual, he shielded these from me behind his own wall of sorrow.

Awaiting me I found a letter from India that did much to dispel such melancholy: it offered a transfer to British horsed cavalry there. The prospect of spending most of the day astride a horse in company with agreeable brother officers appealed, and I accepted with alacrity. To an unattached young man with sporting interest and a thirst for travel the opportunity to participate in the fading glory of empire was all that I aspired to. What I would discover on my journeys through central and northern India was immediately familiar from Kipling's *Kim*, though barely recognisable from Forster's *Passage to India*.

In 1922 the 3rd (Prince of Wales) Dragoon Guards had been amalgamated with the 6th Dragoon Guards, the 'Carabiniers', an honorary title bestowed after the battle of the Boyne. I joined the regiment in October 1937 at Sialkot. The daily routine was to begin schooling polo ponies about six in the morning, then after breakfast parade at the lines at nine o'clock, venture out on troop training, returning about two for a late lunch of coronation chicken. There were polo games on Mondays, Wednesdays and Fridays, and a whole holiday on Thursdays when we went shooting; thus the only possible day one could visit the lines in the afternoon was a Tuesday. If an officer did that, however, his troop sergeant would think he was untrusted.

It was, to say the least, something of a privileged existence that I had done little to merit. Indeed there was a sense of living in a golden time that would never recur: what we had witnessed in Germany had convinced me of that. Perhaps surprisingly the troops reached an advanced state of readiness under this benign regime. But then the Indian Army had had two centuries in which to experiment with training methods.

One day on troop training, Trooper Mulcahy's horse ran away with him and, when asked where he was going, he shouted back, 'I don't know, Sergeant, but the horse comes from Australia.'

Sialkot lies about eighty miles north of Lahore. Beyond the Indian city, the military cantonment occupies about ten square miles of flat plain, with roads laid out on a grid pattern, the barracks to the east and the officers' quarters to the west. It had been built in the 1840s when the East India Company occupied the Punjab after the second Sikh war. Sialkot was one of the flashpoints of the Indian Mutiny, where the commandant and some British officers were murdered. The rebels started to march towards Delhi, but were intercepted and defeated by John Lawrence, who then advanced to Delhi with his force.

Close by, to the east of Sialkot, is the Hindu state of Jammu. To the north, beyond a range of mountains about the size of the Alps, lies Kashmir. In the eighteenth century this was a province of Afghanistan, but at the beginning of the nineteenth the king was expelled from Kabul. He went to the Sikh emperor who ruled the Punjab and ceded Kashmir to him in exchange for his reinstatement to Kabul. This failed, but the Sikhs retained Muslim Kashmir. To pay for the first Sikh war against the East India Company the Sikhs sold Kashmir to the Hindu Maharajah of Jammu. All in all it was a recipe for trouble.

There were only two roads into Kashmir, both across mountain passes. The first, from the south, through Jammu, would be closed by snow in winter, but the road from the west, through the Murree Hills, is always open. So if the partition of India had taken place in winter, the Indian Army could never have reached Kashmir, which they invaded on the basis that although the population was Muslim the ruler was Hindu. Conversely, India took over Hyderabad because the people were Hindu, although the Nizam was Muslim. Naturally the fact that he was then the richest man in the world had nothing to do with it.

The Punjab has a wonderful climate in winter. From mid–September to mid–April the skies are blue and it is pleasantly warm. Then the heat is turned up until mid–July, when the monsoon brings a deluge. In the evenings flying ants would swarm out of the ground to shed their wings into your chota peg (small whisky) as they flew towards the light. It remained scorching and became extremely humid, so that the hot season was continuously unpleasant. A new subaltern arrived as a teetotaller, but did not realise the high cost of fizzy drinks. After his first month, the adjutant said to him, 'We're a hard-drinking regiment, but your bar bill is over the top. Do not let it happen again.' So he changed to chota pegs and there was no further complaint.

In 1937 the Sialkot garrison was occupied by a horsed Indian Cavalry Brigade, consisting of a British regiment and two Indian cavalry regiments, officered principally by Britons. There was also an Indian Infantry battalion and a much-needed hospital. The British regiment maintained a hill station of some charm 4,000 feet up in the Murree Hills, where the families spent the summer, with the troops taking turns there away from the heat. The combination of benign climate, colonial architecture and the view made it an agreeable escape, for which it was worth enduring the sweat of the plains.

The cantonment of Sialkot was laid out as a chequerboard of roads each of which enclosed an acre of land at the officers' end. Every acre lot had a bungalow with four bedrooms, stables and staff quarters. Our bachelors lived four to a bungalow, each employing a bearer and a dogboy, while sharing a gardener, water carrier, sweeper and night watchman. Grooms were also retained, one for each pony. So four subalterns might be employing and housing the families of twenty or more staff on their acre of land.

Everyone had a dog, but some kept other pets. Mine was a mongoose and, for a time, a baby panther. This animal was aware that it terrified Indians, but inspired no fear in a white man. Its eventual growth to full size tested the commandant's tolerance to breaking point, and it was passed to Lahore Zoo. Charles Cubitt kept a bear, Rosie, which he took on a military training course upon which dogs were forbidden.

Service with a British officer was much sought after. We paid above the local rate of employment. My grooms kept their families happily on £1 a month. References were considered essential. One bearer received a reference saying, 'I would give this man a very wide berth.' He took it to a *munshie* (teacher) who told him it meant that he should receive a major posting; somehow, he never got it.

Polo in England was an enjoyable sport amongst many others, but in India it was central. First-class polo was played in the Native States, while in British India there were about twenty Indian Cavalry regiments, and five British, all taking it very seriously. So one played with high-handicap players and learnt some exotic shots. The player on the line of the ball has priority and can place his pony to make the shot unless ridden off by an opponent. In that case the player may be pushed off the line, and the only shot remaining is to lean far forward and strike the ball to the left. If the mallet does not collide with the ponies' legs and bring about a crash, the flexible stick may curl round and strike the opponent on the elbow. This is known as the Millionaire's Shot, and is not recommended.

When playing a back-handed stroke it is dangerous to hit the ball straight back since there is likely to be a player there. It is usual to slice the ball to the right, but also possible to hit the ball behind your pony out to the left. But if your stick hits the pony's tail that tail will clamp down on the stick and the pony will start bucking. You are left stretched back with your wrist attached to the clamped stick, an uncomfortable and ludicrous position. This is known as the 'Buck doesn't stop' stroke.

In the 1930s foul language was not used in front of ladies. But on the polo ground things were different when tempers became heated. Graham Dollar, from my regiment, always managed to deploy his worst oaths as he galloped past where the ladies were seated. The immaculate Peter Dollar, 4th Hussars, was smooth as a cravat and played polo for England. His brother Graham was his exact opposite, except for the polo. When he broke his nose for the second time in a riding accident he did not trouble to have it set again, and in consequence was appallingly ugly, though a lovable eccentric.

You could always tell a cavalry officer's wife by the faraway look in her eyes, caused by watching polo, so frequently played on the far side of the ground. The wife of one seven-handicap player refused to sit with the other wives, but remained with his ponies, so that she could give him earnest advice every time he changed mounts.

One of my first tasks upon arrival in India was to buy some polo ponies, which required sound judgement as there were plenty of duds on offer. I was fortunate to have had the experience of five polo seasons in England, but not every buy proved a success. Penelope was handy and agile, but suffered from a dry mouth, so by the end of a chukka she was uncontrollable. In a tournament, I played her in the first chukka, when I might hope to get away with the ball before anyone else had woken up. As soon as a goal was scored I would gallop off the field and change ponies, jumping from one saddle to the other.

By the outbreak of war I had six ponies. Razzle, like the Maltese cat in Kipling's story, understood and enjoyed polo, but his reins had to be left loose. If I wished to stop at full gallop, I had only to close my legs and lean back. When a backhand shot was made Razzle and I would both know where to go, and I was invariably first on the new line of the ball. He won the cup for the best polo pony in the north of India in 1939.

For long leave, we were given two alternatives: three months every summer, or two months' leave twice followed by six months in the third year. To keep my options open I took two months in 1938 in Kashmir. First I went into the mountains north of the Vale, in pursuit of bear or stag. A message arrived warning that a bear was in the corn and the villagers would beat it out towards my position. In the dusk I raised my rifle as a large dark figure emerged, but it was the village idiot with a blanket over his head, whom I was meant to shoot. This doubtless would have resulted in massive compensation for his family and the village.

One afternoon I was sitting reading in my tent, when I looked down and saw a snake circling round my legs. I do not know which of us was quicker out of that tent. On a similar trek, a man had been bitten in the hand by a snake. With great presence of mind he quickly chopped off the hand at the wrist. He returned to civilization carrying the snake, and they had not the heart to tell him that it was not poisonous.

I then tried fishing, but every time I cast a fly it would at once be snapped up by a large trout, of which there were too many. Finally, I moved on to Gulmarg. The daily routine was a round of golf before lunch, another round after lunch, bridge after tea and a hotel dance following dinner. Here in winter I could pursue my other great passion, skiing. Gulmarg is a flat bowl of open ground on the northern slopes of Mount Afarwat, high above the Vale of Kashmir, then boasting two golf courses and Nedou's Hotel. The Ski Club of India opened it annually for a week over the New Year, with a pony track dug for 1,500 feet to the tree-line at 10,000 feet. You rode your pony up as far as possible, then put on skins and climbed, and finally had a run down to meet your pony at the bottom. I once climbed, somewhat breathlessly, to the summit of 17,000 feet, five hours up and what seemed like five minutes down. On another occasion I saw what seemed to be huge human footprints running diagonally downhill, so I followed them until the gradient changed, and the bear no longer put his back foot just ahead of the snow print of his forefoot. Not surprisingly Yeti 'sightings' were regularly reported. I attended this ski meeting each year from 1938 to 1941 and organised an inter-regimental relay race, with teams of three, which was probably the first British Army ski race held anywhere.

In 1938 the adjutant returned from leave in England with a new and nervous bride. I attended their first dinner party with the Brigade Commander and our second-in-command and their wives. At dinner, the second's wife got very drunk and insisted that the exotic Anglo-Indian actress Merle Oberon was a Calcutta tart. When the ladies retired to the drawing room she proved that she could stand on her head, thereby demonstrating that she was not wearing knickers. At that moment the *abdar* entered to serve coffee and, rather naturally, dropped the tray. We went on to watch *Gone with the Wind*, but the second-in-command took his wife home.

The second-in-command had been a fighter pilot in 60 Squadron, Royal Flying Corps, in the First World War. One morning, Billy Bishop, the Canadian ace, woke him to say, 'I'm going to win a Victoria Cross before breakfast.' He did, and was back for breakfast. Bishop had made an unexpected attack on a German fighter airfield, and destroyed ten Fokkers.

On guest nights we had the unusual tradition, not only of not standing for 'God Save the King' but of continuing to talk through it, which takes some doing. This was occasioned by the Prince Regent, too drunk to stand up, saying, 'Gentlemen, I don't doubt your loyalty, so take no notice of this.' His father, George III, suffering from insanity, had been in no position to object.

Behaviour in the officers' mess on guest nights was always boisterous, and I became the acknowledged expert at debagging, which was achieved by first unbuttoning a victim's back braces. We also played a popular game known as aeroplanes, which consisted of taking a running dive over two armchairs placed together, and landing with a neck-roll on a sofa strategically placed. Many years later, in 1966, while on a parliamentary visit to Germany, I dined with my old regiment and a quiet game of cards was proposed for the after-dinner entertainment, so I reintroduced aeroplanes with a demonstration.

As the senior amalgamated cavalry regiment, we had been promised that we would be the last to be mechanised, but this undertaking was forgotten and we were ordered to start mechanisation with the Vickers light tank on 1st January 1938. This was a most unwelcome development as the introduction of tanks was considered to be quite disastrous for men trained to ride into battle on horseback. Of course, such modernisation was inevitable, but that did not make it any more acceptable. When the 13/18th Hussars left for England Tony Stocker bequeathed me his bearer, reputed to be the best in India. He had been with Tony when he was ADC to the Viceroy and was most supportive.

One Saturday evening at the Sialkot Officers Club, a group of us were having a convivial evening, and started some mischief to help club funds, because the rule was that damages had to be paid for at three times replacement cost. Captain Lister, of the Tank Regiment, attached to the regiment to help us mechanise, called for a hammer and nail, then signed a chit saying 'I did this' and nailed it to the plate-glass top of the bar, which of course shattered.

At the time it seemed extremely funny, but the next morning the club secretary took a different view. He invited the garrison commander, Brigadier Tom Corbett (later a lieutenant general) to inspect the attempt to ruin the club facilities. Corbett undertook to deal with the ringleader. Lister was the senior officer present, but being a sort of guest, could not be considered the ringleader: thus the honour fell to me.

Corbett assembled the commanding officers to decide a suitable punishment, when Lieutenant Colonel Frank Messervy, then commanding the 13th Lancers, asked if they all had not committed a similar prank when young. I received a light rebuke, but we still paid for the damage three times over.

In 1939 I decided to take three months' leave. I travelled home by Imperial Airways flying boat. The first leg was from Karachi to Basra. The next day we were due to reach Alexandria, but headwinds over the desert forced us to stop at Lake Tiberias. Palestine was experiencing a revolt, so a military guard was put aboard the flying boat, whose use of the lights drained the batteries. We were not allowed to go sightseeing while the batteries were recharged, but had to remain in the hotel. That afternoon we flew only to Alexandria so the journey home took five, instead of four days. By contrast, I returned to India by KLM Dakota, taking just three days from Amsterdam. We were due at Karachi at 4 p.m., and the clock was striking four as we landed.

I arrived home in time for the last day of the season's hunting with the Warwickshire. I was mounted on my father's new hunter, Weedon, a splendid jumper. Hounds found a fox on the far side of the Evenlode brook, so the huntsman jumped it and so did I, but the rest of the field went off for a mile to find a bridge. Weedon then went out to grass as a six-year-old and stayed there until I returned in 1945, when he showed no signs of being any older.

As the hunting season had ended I took the opportunity of another three weeks in Bill Bracken's racing class at Scheidegg, and on Easter Monday we took the early train to the summit of the Jungfrau, arriving at dawn. Jimmy Gardiner and the celebrated 'Filthy' Fox were going to ski down the Jungfrau glacier, a route never before attempted. Their guide broke a ski early on, but scrambled down just as quickly. We were skiing forty miles to the east, up and down glaciers and over passes, but we knew they had made it when Jimmy flew his aircraft over us on his way back to England. Arnold Lunn wrote this up as a great example of the courage of British youth, mainly to annoy Hitler. I doubt this had much impact on the Führer, but war was looming in Europe, and I was to return to my regiment.

3

The War in India

The Second World War found my regiment trained and equipped with light tanks, but with absolutely nowhere to go. We had hoped to be transferred to Egypt, then under threat, and anticipation rose when an important cipher message arrived. When decoded it read, 'HRH will only drink Booth's Gin', referring to a forthcoming visit by the Duke of Gloucester. It was frustrating to be professional soldiers, but apparently unwanted. When war broke out, I considered how it might affect me. If I were not killed, I might lose a limb, but which should it be? Most important was to be able to ride and ski, so I needed both legs, thus the left arm seemed most expendable. Here I was dead right, because Lord Cowdray, thus handicapped, was able to hunt, shoot, fish and, most notably, to play polo. For his seventieth birthday his family gave him a salver with his four sports engraved upon it. When I teased him that they were polo, polo, polo and polo, he indignantly denied it.

One diversion was mental exercise, and in 1940 I heard of the Bagnold Sun Compass, used for the navigation of vehicles in the Western Desert. We had experienced the same difficulties in using a magnetic compass inside a large ferrous object, so I invented a version which was very simple to use, and the Allason Sun Compass was adopted for the Indian Army.

In that year I was appointed the regiment's adjutant. My first challenge arose when a young brother officer began an affair with the wife of an Indian cavalry officer serving overseas. I told him to end it, and he was furious. But the marriage was saved, and after the war he warmly thanked me.

As adjutant, I had to prosecute in any courts-martial. When the troops heard that one of our Emergency Commissioned Officers (ECOs) was a barrister they always asked for him to defend them. They were not aware that Robert Furtado specialised in Income Tax law, and had seldom appeared in court. I never lost a case to him.

Early in the war, I had a recurring dream, always the same, of an aeroplane with a friend on board, crashing in front of me. As I ran to get him out the plane exploded. Then it really happened. A light aircraft was being used to take up our officers, one by one, to gain experience of reconnaissance. Coming in to land with Tom Dimsdale aboard it crashed, but there was no explosion and I managed to pull Tom out. I never had the dream again.

We had posted to us as regimental medical officer a most charming man, Ted Hayward. He had been chief medical officer in Jodhpur state, where his duties included supervision of the state prison. One inmate was causing considerable trouble, so Ted informed him that he was clearly mad, and must be moved to the psychiatric wing. There prisoners were chained, spread-eagled on the floor, which was rarely washed, amid an appalling stench and much screaming. After a month of this the tough prisoner pleaded his sanity and obedience.

Ted assembled the regiment for a lecture on venereal disease so graphic in its detail that three tough troopers fainted. Such was his enjoyment of army life that he stayed on after the war as Surgeon Major of the Royal Horse Guards. We remained friends for the rest of his life.

As regulars we were initially in awe of the businessmen who arrived as emergency commissioned officers, but the only brilliant brain that I encountered belonged to Major Harry Fisher, son of the Archbishop of Canterbury. I found myself obliged to reprimand him for being ostentatiously efficient. The worst ECO I met was a subaltern so wet and incompetent that I could not understand why he had been commissioned; the only excuse seemed to be that he had been at Eton. I reported that if he were an other rank he would not have made lance corporal. He was transferred as a private in a line regiment. Later he was seen in Burma. His commander said he had been made company runner, as he could not be trusted with a rifle.

When the previous adjutant had been approached with a problem, he would tell the person concerned to return after five minutes while he considered the issue. I scorned the subterfuge, and would call in the orderly room quartermaster sergeant (ORQMS), who knew King's Regulations by heart. He always had a solution to every problem, and

I was conscious that he was probably officer material. We were asked to recommend warrant officers for commissions, and all of ours were worthy, but the colonel complained that if the ORQMS left, the regiment would collapse. I said the ORQMS must not be penalised for his own efficiency, and we duly managed without him. I was delighted when he reached the rank of lieutenant colonel ahead of me. When our officers' mess sergeant was running General Bill Slim's mess at 14th Army as a major, Lord Louis Mountbatten tried to poach him with the offer of promotion, but he remained loyal to Slim.

In 1941 we were asked if the regiment could provide the essential posts to form another regiment, receiving drafts from British infantry battalions in India. We accepted the challenge and the 25th Dragoons were formed under our second-in-command. A complaint was made to GHQ about the criminals sent by a Scottish battalion, but their indignant colonel was able to plead that he had sent his best men. The losses from the regiment meant promotion for those remaining, and I was appointed a squadron-leader.

That year, as a youthful-looking major, I consulted an Indian fortune teller. Mistaking the crown on my shoulder for a single pip, he informed me that I would soon be a full lieutenant, which was not welcome news. He went on to say that I would go to hospital and have a long sea voyage, a forecast which would apply to most British soldiers in India, but I was one of the very few who returned to England by air during the war, rather than on a troopship. He was possibly not in the first rank of his profession.

In March 1942 Gulmarg had a special opening for Easter skiing and I was invited, together with two brother officers, to join the two daughters of the Viceroy, Joan and Bunty Hope and his daughter-in-law, Viv Hopetown, with all of whom we got on tremendously well. Lord Linlithgow's daughters were unkindly labelled 'Faint Hope, Little Hope and No Hope'. Faint Hope had already married. Little Hope, Lady Joan Hope, was very tall and had a voice which was off-putting until you got to know her well. No Hope, Lady Doreen Hope, or Bunty, had a bulbous nose and a bulbous shape, but was immensely jolly. If a dance band played a Swiss waltz she and I would stick our bottoms out and whirl around, and our combined twenty-five stone would knock all other couples off the dance floor. Viv, the Countess of Hopetown, in contrast, was petite and quite beautiful. Joan and Bunty both married after the war, Bunty to Brigadier Erroll Prior Palmer. Their daughter Lucinda became an Olympic Equestrian champion.

Skiing together at Gulmarg that Easter the sun was so fierce that we would climb on hard crust in the morning until it began to melt, and then have one run in wonderful spring snow before lunchtime. After lunch we would climb through slush until it started to freeze, when we had another fine run home. One afternoon I arranged what we called a 'fox hunt'. As fox, I skied to a V-shaped col, down one side, and up the other. Then, as the pack followed, I went down and up the first side. We achieved a lot of skiing, with varying abilities all being catered for.

We composed couplets about each other. Joan's one about me was 'M is for major, too foxy for words, who skis quite divinely and makes paper birds'. The last bit refers to the origami that I made for Viv's small daughter.

Light tanks were proving useless in Burma, and it was not at all clear that there was a role for armour in the jungle. How could we be deployed usefully when we were equipped with armour quite unsuited for combat in the very environment chosen by the Japanese? The American Stuart, which had replaced our Vickers, was not much better, proving difficult to manoeuvre despite rubber tracks. With the governor removed my squadron commander's tank could reach sixty-five miles per hour, forward and in reverse. When the Americans entered the war in December 1941, and flooded into India to find us still playing polo, they were scornful. I asked one so expressing himself whether he had ever had a wall blown on top of him by a German bomb, which shut him up. Happily he had not pressed me on the detail of my close encounter with the enemy, and he was left with the definite impression that I had endured the Blitz.

By 1943 the Japanese, seemingly invincible, had reached the borders of India. This certainly caused alarm in Calcutta, chiefly from fear of bombing, but to those of us five hundred miles away there seemed no threat, in such a vast subcontinent. The Congress party proclaimed a 'Quit India campaign of non-co-operation', but to little effect. The steel industry, a major contributor to Congress funds, explained that it was doing too well to cease production, while the peasantry proved uninterested, preferring good government with the minimum of corruption. The enormous Indian Army remained as brave and loyal as ever.

The Americans took the 'Quit India' campaign more seriously and hopefully. Perhaps America could supplant British business in India? When a photograph appeared of Gandhi visiting his British dentist in Bombay in a Rolls-Royce decorated with a 'Quit India' placard, the Americans mistook this for British subservence. They did not see that it was the British laughing at the hypocrisy of a man enjoying the luxury of British services while urging others to boycott them. The police experienced some difficulty interning Congress troublemakers, but the general Indian population showed no hostility to the British. The most serious blow in 1943 was the loss of imports of rice from Burma, causing famine in Bengal, where the rice eaters were unable to adapt to any alternative offered such as flour.

The Stuart light tank having proved useless in Burma, we moved to Secunderabad, near Hyderabad, to train with Grant medium tanks. The Nizam of Hyderabad's forces were around, and polo was still played. I had kept the best three of my ponies. The Nizam's son, the Prince of Berar, a flabby creature, used to put his name down to play polo each day but invariably was taken ill at the last moment. When our regimental polo team played a match against Hyderabad State forces, for a war charity in front of a huge crowd, I was relied on to score some goals as I was the best-mounted player on our side. However, in the very first chukka, their back backhanded the ball dangerously straight back, and it struck my right arm above the elbow. Thereafter I could only swing my polo stick with a straight arm. Our reserve player played my pony in the second chukka, but could not manage it, so I played the last two chukkas. We were hopelessly defeated and the Princess of Berar petulantly refused to present the prizes.

While the regiment was at Secunderabad, the Duke of Gloucester paid us another visit. My squadron of Grant tanks was thirty miles away on jungle warfare training, but I was instructed to bring it back. I explained that my tanks had an allocation of 100 miles of track mileage for training for a whole year, so if I brought them in we would lose sixty miles of training. The commanding officer, Derek Schreiber, a spit-and-polish fanatic, glared up with the words, 'Did you not hear my order, Allason?'

I am sure the Duke was happier with his Booth's gin in the mess than seeing my thirteen tanks gleaming in line with all the others. He might have been more interested to see the Grants training in the jungle. At that time it had not been realised that the three-inch gun in the hull was the best means of destroying Japanese bunkers.

Later on, during the battle of the Box, one of my tanks was hit by a shell which failed to penetrate. The tank commander got out to inspect the damage. Remarkably he was not fired upon, perhaps because the enemy did not want to disclose their position when there was a 1.3-inch turret gun and co-axial Browning machine gun pointing in their general direction. The tank commander examined the groove in the armour and calculated where the shot must have come from. A few rounds from the three-inch gun destroyed the Japanese gun and its bunker.

For Christmas 1942 I was invited to the Viceroy's house in Delhi, where I was intrigued to see the imposing Marquess of Linlithgow, before whom even the most powerful maharajahs quaked, unbend into a jolly family man, pulling crackers. Royal etiquette was observed by the household and before each dinner party the guests lined up as the Viceroy and Vicereine entered and shook hands with everyone, before leading us into the dining room.

This followed the Christmas-morning service at the Cathedral of the Redemption during which the family, whose patronymic was Hope, had to endure a lengthy sermon by the Metropolitan of India attacking the Viceroy's attitude to Congress and Home Rule. The peroration of the sermon led to gales of laughter as the verbose Metropolitan gestured towards the front pew with the words, "and all we have left is an array of blasted Hopes'.

Linlithgow had held the post since 1936 and would do so until the following year, 1943, the longest period served by any Viceroy. He proved a wily statesman, and more than a match for the Indian nationalists upon whose vanity he played. A dinner invitation to one of the leaders, to whom he would listen attentively, could be guaranteed to produce a fissure within the movement. Such was his power that within hours of Neville Chamberlain declaring war upon Germany Linlithgow had, without consulting a single Indian, felt able to follow suit on behalf of India. It was apparent that he was a realist with a longer vision than that possessed by many of the politicians at home. His adoption of a federal form of government had already furthered the cause of Indian independence, although by the date of my visit his priorities had become the suppression of opposition to Britain from nationalists and the organisation of India's hostilities with Japan. Politics apart, the feat that impressed me was the duck shoot in which he told me he had participated at Keoladeo in Rajasthan in November 1938: the bag had totalled 4,273 birds.

Tact has never been one of my salient qualities. I related to Lord Linlithgow an extract from one of Saki's short stories, 'The Jesting of Arlington Stringham', the punchline of which was, 'My aunt has even been known to learn humility from a Viceroy'. This evidently struck home, because he enquired of a daughter, 'You don't think I'm pompous, do you?' Saki was, of course, referring to Lord Curzon.

When Curzon was Viceroy in Calcutta, he built a replica of his home, Keddleston Hall. It later became the home of the Governor of Bengal. Earlier in the war I had been in Calcutta with a brother officer, Edward Sandford, and we went to call on his aunt, Lady Herbert, the wife of the Governor. We brought along a new toy just arrived, a Jeep, and drove it up the steps and into the Blue Drawing room. I doubt if Curzon would have approved.

The Viceroy's House in Delhi, designed by Lutyens to impress, was so large that it was a lengthy walk from my bedroom to breakfast. The Duke of Gloucester used a bicycle. With 340 rooms and a floor area of 200,000 square feet, it was little surprise to discover that the number of employees working within it and tending the gardens exceeded two thousand. The palace was laid out around a great quadrangle off which radiated government buildings, forming a single nexus of power in which head of state and executive entwined without recourse to legislature.

The Viceroy and his family occupied the centre building, a four-storey house so large than no president of India has since felt comfortable enough to occupy it, although it remains their official residence. I was quartered in the guest wing. Occupying the centre of the main part of the palace was the throne room, with thrones for the Viceroy and Vicereine positioned beneath the great dome. Suspended from a 100-foot chain was a chandelier weighing two tons. The effect was austere but undeniably impressive. Through the loggias and halls the Viceroy glided serenely, a living embodiment of empire, imposing even to those who worked closely with him.

After this memorable Christmas I was sent to the Staff College, Quetta, arriving in January 1943, accompanied by my three polo ponies. Besides playing polo three days a week, they raced in the weekly

Quetta handicap races on Saturdays, which, to my surprise did them no harm.

It was while at Staff College that it was inculcated into me that there are four sorts of officer: the idle and inefficient; the hard-working and efficient; the idle but efficient; and the hard-working but inefficient. The latter are really dangerous, but it is the third category that rises to the top. To prove my idleness, I regularly played bridge far into the night, and made a lifelong friend in Jai, the Maharajah of Jaipur, who was on the same course.

There were two commandos participating in the programme. Major Bill Seymour, Scots Guards, had been chased out of Burma by the Japanese. When they reached Mandalay, everyone turned left and had a terrible trek over mountainous jungle to reach India. Except Bill, who turned right and walked into China, where his uncle was British Ambassador. On his first night in Chunking he found himself seated at dinner on the right of Madame Chiang Kai-Shek. He was offered a dish of fish, so took a slice with his chopsticks, but the slice started to slip. Instead of letting it fall back on the dish, he made a grab for it. Madame was wearing a very low-cut dress, and that was where the fish went.

The other commando was possessed of less charm. When asked why he had come to the Staff College, he said it was to learn the dirty tricks of the staff. This did not endear him to the directing officers, and I doubt he received a good posting.

When I met an old friend who was going to the Staff College Camberley, at the end of 1945, I warned him against it. Brigadier Mike Calvert, a hero of the Chindit special forces, who had led his brigade headquarters staff in bayonet charges against the Japanese, would, I feared, be the target for jealousy. Sure enough, at the end of his course he was given a major's posting in Yugoslavia.

Happily, the Maharajah of Jaipur had brought some of his own polo ponies to Quetta and we had many enjoyable games of polo before Jai had to be recalled to his state just before the end of the course rather than fail. He unquestionably fell into the first category of officers. An instructor on the course was one of General Bernard Montgomery's brothers. He told me that in 1937, when Monty's wife had died following an infected insect bite, the general had taken to the bottle so severely that his doctor told him to give it up or die. This, according to his brother, was the reason for Monty's famous abstinence.

Jai Man Singh, the sporting Maharajah of Jaipur, and his wife Gayatri Devi, known to family and friends as Ayesha.

Rambagh Palace, Jaipur. Jai usually managed to make himself comfortable.

Photo by Julian Allason

The Chamber of Princes with the Viceroy: more than just a talking shop.

4

GHQ India

At the end of the course, I was given the plum posting to the Joint Planning Staff in Delhi, very much at the centre of war preparations. Very soon we needed another planner of General Staff Officer 2 (GSO2) seniority, because one of us had to fly to a conference at Calcutta, and I lost the toss. The aircraft carrying my colleague exploded in mid-air, killing all aboard. As a consequence I was asked to suggest a replacement from my course, and Dmitri Zvegintzov of the Border Regiment proved a complete success.

While in Delhi I kept just one pony, and cantered to work every morning wearing leather riding chaps, followed by my syce or groom on my bicycle. When we reached the entrance to GHQ, we swapped mounts. This was my main opportunity for exercise, although after work I had an open invitation to use the Viceroy's swimming pool. As our friendship developed, based on our shared Staff College experience, Jai invited me to stay the weekend at his palace in Jaipur. It was a ceremonial weekend with elephant processions. Jai realised that I would have preferred sport, so he suggested my staying on over Monday, promising me a very full schedule. In the morning we would drive for tiger mounted on elephants, over lunch shoot crocodile from an electric canoe. Next came hyena bashing, when you ride after the beast with a polo ball fixed to the end of a polo stick, and play polo shots at it (it was a mistake to fall off). After a game of polo there would be fights between wild beasts. Unfortunately, I was working on an urgent plan in Delhi, and had to decline these Indian Olympics.

In 1939 Jai had married Princess Gayatri Devi of Cooch Behar, a classical beauty possessed of considerable independence of mind and a delightfully dry sense of humour. Ayesha, as she was known to friends, had been educated partly in Europe and was a fine rider. She was not to be confined to the purdah in which Jai's first two wives lived. Indeed she would be instrumental in its abolition, when she later became a politician, being elected with the largest majority ever recorded in a democratic election. She and Jai were to figure in my life for many years to come.

One memorable evening a party rode out to a moonlight picnic at a Moghul tomb outside Delhi. I was riding home with a rather beautiful girl when a downpour started. She was wearing a white shirt and jodhpurs, and I wore a bush hat, checked shirt and chaps. We saw lights at a bungalow nearby and rode in for shelter from the storm. It was an American officers' mess, and the occupants might have been forgiven for thinking Hedy Lamarr and Gary Cooper had ridden in out of the rain.

Britain only ruled about one-half of the subcontinent directly. The remainder was reigned over by a pantheon of Indian princes, maharajahs (great ruler) or rajahs, who ruled territories varying from the size of Wales to just a few square miles. Each was guided by a British Resident, there to see that they did not step out of line. Some rulers bore exotic titles, such as the Nizam of Hyderabad or the Gaekwar of Baroda.

One morning my telephone rang and an awed operator put through 'His Highness of Jaipur'. He had discovered that we were both trying to give drinks parties on the same evening, and as many of the same names were likely to appear on each guestlist, we had better combine. I realised he was referring to the Viceroy's family, but objected that I had a number of guests that he did not know. This was hardly an obstacle to a prince. As usual Jai's hospitality proved fulsome, even if it was my guests who stayed on the longest. We ended in the private railway carriage of a maharajah at 2 a.m.

I was able to make some recompense a few years later, when Jai's son, Jagat, was at Harrow. In the holidays when he could not join his parents he came to stay with us, and became a great friend of my two sons, sharing Julian's photographic studio in the attic, up the stairs to which a succession of beauties traipsed. Whilst he was Prince Jagat of Jaipur, he enjoyed unlimited credit in Bond Street, but when Mrs Gandhi, Prime Minister of India, abolished the princely titles, Mr Jagat Singh found he did not get quite the same treatment.

In Delhi I encountered the sumptuously attired Jam Sahib of Nawanagar, who collected precious stones, not to decorate his wives but as others collect stamps. When the Jonkers diamond was discovered just before the war, it was brought to him uncut: he had no interest in uncut stones however. Instead it was bought by an American syndicate, who then employed an American rather than a Dutchman to cut it, and he had only practised for a year before doing so. They again brought it to the Jam Sahib, who rolled it in the palm of his hand and saw at once that one face was flawed. So he refused to buy. He told them he would have given a million pounds for it otherwise. 'I hope that was a lesson to them', he chortled.

Son of the famous cricketer, Ranji, the Jam Sahib's interests were not purely narcissistic. At that time, he was supporting in his state, at his own expense, five thousand Polish orphan refugee children, who had been expelled from Siberia by Stalin. The Jam Sahib is remembered and loved in Poland to this day, and descendants of those children still visit India, preserving an improbable bond of affection.

One day a short burly figure slunk into my office and demanded to see the plans for Burma. The uniform proclaimed him a lieutenant-colonel in the Royal Warwickshire Regiment, but he had a yellow face, crew-cut hair and a thin toothbrush moustache. He did not seem to know a soul in the Warwicks, so I was suspicious, but my GSO1 came in and promptly showed him the plans. As soon as our visitor left, I voiced concern that he might be a Japanese spy, so we had the gates locked while he was checked. The officer turned out to be the brilliant young classics professor, Enoch Powell, recovering from jaundice on his meteoric rise from the rank of private to brigadier, and our new intelligence liaison officer. At our conferences, when he should have remained silent until asked, he interrupted and interfered, contradicting whoever was speaking. It was clear he had to go, but it needed to be upwards, so he was promoted full colonel. Our paths were to cross again.

In mid-1943 we had little to show for the fight in Burma, where the Japanese had consolidated their positions. The exponent of guerrilla warfare, Brigadier Orde Wingate, had led a force of picked men behind enemy lines without doing much damage to the Japanese, but had sustained appalling casualties. Wingate had gained a reputation as a swashbuckling adventurer earlier in the war, organising small raiding parties in the Sudan. Despite a gift for proselytising ideas of unconventional warfare his personal habits were eccentric; he often wore an alarm clock on his wrist and consumed raw onions. His inclination to nudism was made even less aesthetic by the substitution of a rubdown with a rubber brush for bathing. Not everyone had been impressed with Wingate's unorthodox guerrilla tactics, and doubts arose about his mental stability after he had attempted to cut his own throat in a Cairo hotel but, as a mutual friend remarked to me, 'He made a mess of it as usual.'

The Commander-in-Chief, General Claude Auchinleck, told him he was a failure, and that he would be sent home, but as we could not admit another failure, he would be given good publicity. Unfortunately Winston Churchill, ever on the look-out for a short-cut to victory, took the misleading news coverage at face value and we received a signal from the chiefs of staff about a plan dreamed up by Wingate to capture Sumatra. We knew that the real chiefs of staff were in mid-Atlantic on their way to the Ottawa Conference with the North American Allies, and concluded that the signal had come from the second eleven in London, so our reply was rather dismissive. Back came a signal: 'Personal from Prime Minister: General Wingate will return to lead large force in Burma.'

The Ottawa Conference produced a major upheaval, with Lord Louis Mountbatten, formerly the Chief of Combined Operations, being appointed Supreme Allied Commander, South-East Asia, to direct operations in Burma, with Lieutenant-General Sir George Giffard as Army Group Commander, instead of leaving operational responsibility at GHQ in Delhi. Accordingly, our planning staff transferred to South-East Asia Command, and our plans for operations in early 1944 were amended to include an ambitious operation by Wingate. When Wingate fell ill, and Mountbatten visited him in hospital, the supremo asked if he had everything he needed. 'I want an air force,' was the startling reply, and he got one.

The Americans were impressed with Wingate, and gave him an air commando with fighters and transports, for his exclusive use. It was commanded by Colonel 'Flip' Cochrane, with Lieutenant-Colonel Alison as his second-in-command, with whom I had to deal; this offered plentiful opportunities for confusion. The final plan involved two brigades who were to march in to operate behind enemy lines, with a third being inserted by glider. Alison explained to me that the Dakotas could tug two gliders each, even over the turbulent Chin Hills, and after landing the gliders could be snatched off the strip and returned to base. This advice proved to be ill-founded, but he bamboozled me into lending him every glider we had.

In Delhi Wingate had suggested that when in Burma he should capture a town of no importance, then announce it as second only to Mandalay, so that the Japanese would lose face unless they recaptured it. An Indian division should then be flown in to garrison it and kill off hundreds of Japanese. Such a hare-brained scheme was completely impractical, and the plan was turned down, but never abandoned by Wingate and his staff. Some of the support he did receive was attributable to Mountbatten's taste for the flamboyant and unconventional, just as he had warmed to Wingate personally.

Mountbatten cut a dashing, if theatrical figure, part Nelson, part HMS Pinafore. 'Never knowingly under-dressed', was my diary note, though I confided none of my reservations in letters home to my sister or father who was now commanding the county's Home Guard. Imbued with energy, enthusiasm and personal courage, Mountbatten was used to getting his way, and prepared to deploy his considerable personal charm to achieve it. While this lubricated relations with Churchill and Eden, his most constant supporters in the War Cabinet, it was not enough to win the unqualified respect of the three groups best able to assess his judgement: his generals, his planners and the American commanders. The attrition rate was high: in 1944 he lost within a few months his deputy, his chief of staff, deputy chief of staff and all three commanders in chief.

As planners we were, necessarily, among the best informed in the headquarters, with access to current dispositions and all the latest intelligence. The breaking of Japanese military and diplomatic ciphers had given us insight into their strategic thinking that Burma represented a vital bulwark against Allied expansion from India – but little cheer as they continued to consolidate their grip. The four divisions with which they had taken the country were progressively reinforced, and would reach a total of eight by March 1944.

Despite the fiasco of the August 1942 Dieppe raid, in which more than half of the invading force and 119 of our aircraft were lost, Mountbatten seemed to have learned little from his time as Chief of Combined Operations when he had pushed it through despite Montgomery's opposition. Now Mountbatten was set on launching a Combined Operations landing somewhere in the region. The Prime

Minister wanted to humour him, so he was promised landing craft for March 1944 and, as a result, we on the planning staff were ordered to plan the capture of the Andaman Islands.

This was to be a major strategic move, but Peter Fleming, the former explorer now in charge of deception, objected to me that he had just persuaded the Japanese that we intended to undertake this very operation, and that the enemy had taken Fleming's warning seriously. His objective had been to identify somewhere completely worthless, and then persuade the enemy that it was strategically very significant, so that they would waste troops and equipment defending it. Indeed, Fleming revealed that his hoax had been so successful that the Japanese had even managed to base fighter planes on the main island by digging tunnels to provide sufficient length for separate take-off and landing strips. To have any hope of victory in an assault that would be heavily opposed, we estimated that we would have to land two well-trained divisions in a very unpleasant and uncertain venture.

I was obliged to work closely with Fleming, whose family we knew. Fleming's mother Eve was an amorous widow, having been Augustus John's mistress, and later living with an impecunious and very elderly peer, Henry Winchester. As for the urbane and handsome Peter, he was undoubtedly one of his brother Ian's models for James Bond, and was married to Celia Johnson, one of the most glamorous actresses of the time. I was aware that he had been accompanied on one of his expeditions by the distinguished explorer Freya Stark, although her presence seemed to have been overlooked in the accounts of the pre-war travels across the globe which had made his reputation. If he had a tendency to embroider, this was precisely the skill needed in the field of deception, so Peter had undoubtedly found his niche.

Fortunately, soon afterwards the offer of landing craft was withdrawn, and to our relief the operation was cancelled, due to the overriding need for such vessels in Europe. Mountbatten, of course, was furious, and in his memoirs he expressed bitter regret at the loss of the operation. It was due to take place in April 1944 just as the critical battle of Kohima, the 'Stalingrad of the East', was about to begin, when those two divisions were desperately needed to repel Japanese attempts to capture Kohima ridge which dominated our supply routes.

As things turned out, the strong Japanese garrison did no harm to anyone for three years in which they occupied the Andamans, having been effectively neutralised there. This must have been the most effective strategic deception plan in the Burma campaign.

Brigadier Walter Cawthorne was the Director of Military Intelligence, India, and bore the heavy responsibility of managing the collection of intelligence in Burma. Suddenly, with the creation of SEAC, he found himself honourably relieved of this role and was looking forward to being able to relax at long last. Following Enoch Powell's appointment as full colonel as his deputy, however, poor Cawthorne had no peace, coping with constant suggestions from the dynamic and ambitious Enoch, who was eventually moved elsewhere and promoted again, this time to Brigadier.

5

Burma

The British plan for the 1944 Burma campaign was to attack in the Arakan in the north-east in January and from our base in the Indian town of Imphal in March. Curiously enough, the Japanese had exactly the same ideas. They attacked in the Arakan one day before our offensive was due. The Japanese plan was derived from their experience that when the British were encircled, they would fight their way out and retire to a fresh position further back. So in the Arakan, their aim was to surround one division so that the hole punched in the Corps line would trigger a long retreat. With luck, this might also cause the committal of the British strategic reserve. But for an effective invasion of India to be achieved, 4 Corps must first be dislodged from Imphal. From there the road into Assam would provide the Japanese with access to the Assam railway. If this could be reached, all supplies to the American forces in North Assam and China could be cut off. China might then be obliged to negotiate a peace.

The Japanese also believed that India was in a state of virtual insurrection, and that the slightest pressure on the British would force a withdrawal. In this the Japanese had been persuaded by the Indian nationalist leader Subhas Chandra Bhose that the population was ready for revolution. In reality Bhose had been encouraged to believe this by his success in recruiting the three hundred or so members of the so-called Indian National Army who, not unnaturally, had preferred to adopt the guise of disloyalty to the empire rather than face the privations of being a prisoner of war in Singapore.

In the Arakan, however, the Indian Division stood their ground when encircled, and were supplied by air drops for three weeks until the Japanese had to pull back. In March, the Japanese encircled 4 Corps at Imphal, but the defenders also stayed to fight it out, supplied by air for the next three months. Air supply had come a long way since its first military use in 1934 in the Chaco War between Bolivia and Paraguay, when the Bolivian commander, General Estikavera, had his champagne flown in to his mountain headquarters, and magnanimously permitted the wounded to use the plane on the return journey.

Halfway between Imphal and the base on the railway at Sylhet the road crosses a ridge running for about a mile between two mountains, at Kohima. Soon after the siege of Imphal began, a Japanese division emerged from the jungle after a long march. The garrison of Kohima consisted of one British battalion and about two thousand Indians in various units. The non-combatants were sent away and the remainder manned the ridge, so the Japanese were obliged to launch a frontal assault. So close was the engagement that at the District Commissioner's tennis court, carved out of the hillside, the foes were dug in on either side.

Incredibly, the position was held for fourteen days before relief arrived in the form of 2nd British Division, which would then have been in the Andaman Islands had Mountbatten had his way. The Japanese were now placed on the defensive, but could not be dislodged until a further division, 7th Indian from the Arakan, took a leaf out of the Japanese book and encircled the enemy. Only then did the remnants of the enemy force fade away into the jungle.

The two divisions then fought their way through a series of Japanese defences to relieve Imphal. Little did they know that they had embarked on a journey that would take them to Rangoon. When the 1944 monsoon broke the 14th Army found itself back at square one after a great victory. Stilwell had reopened the land route to China.

In April 1944, the Chindits had three brigades based on airstrips near the railway running north of Myitkyina. They had some effect on the Japanese line of supply into Myitkyina, but Bernard Fergusson's brigade had been behind enemy lines for three months, and was now flown out. Calvert and Master's brigades moved north to help at Myitkyina. On the way, Calvert captured the town of Mogaung. When he heard on the radio that the Americans had done it, he signalled, 'If the Americans have taken Mogaung, I have taken umbrage', which had the Americans searching their maps.

Independently from 14th Army, the Americans had a base at Ledo, in North Assam, whence supplies were flown into China. From Ledo, in the north-east corner of India, a road runs south to Myitkyina in Burma, at the southern end of a huge mountain range. Thence the road turns east to China. This corner of the world, where three countries met, had thus acquired a strategic importance as a route along which the Americans had been able to truck supplies to General Chiang Kai-Shek in Chunking until prevented by the Japanese invasion. Since then all supplies had to be flown over the 'hump', a uniquely dangerous undertaking in extremely unpredictable and hazardous weather conditions.

General 'Vinegar Joe' Stilwell, America's second most senior commander, was advancing south from Ledo with two Chinese divisions, furious at being left in a backwater while his juniors were gaining fame in Europe. Relations between Giffard and Stilwell, who was also Deputy Supreme Allied Commander, were strained. Stilwell was a small wiry man whose eyes were often masked by dark glasses; polite conversation formed no part of his armoury. The Chinese troops were reluctant to engage the Japanese, but preferred to disappear into the jungle, except when they were personally led by Stilwell, a not infrequent occurrence. The British rated him a good and brave company commander.

Giffard had spent most of his service in Africa, and had no experience of the Indian Army, but he was a most charming man, if not exactly a snappy dresser. Neither were qualities calculated to impress Stilwell. In January 1944 General Giffard was making a tour of the front, so I arranged to accompany him, with an attachment to 14th Army Headquarters at the end of the tour to gain close knowledge of the fight against the Japanese. On the first leg of our journey we flew to Ledo in a draughty old unarmed, twin-engined Anson and lost an engine when we hit a buzzard as we came in to land. The Americans had difficulty believing that this was a four-star general emerging from the rickety aircraft. We had timed our arrival to see off Brigadier Bernard Fergusson, then in command of the first of the Chindit brigades to enter Burma that year. Just after our arrival there was an air-raid warning, and three American fighters roared down the runway together to take off. A Dakota was coming in to land in the opposite direction and had to bank sharply to avoid them. It must have been empty, as it did not fall out of the sky.

We had dinner with Fergusson in a Chinese restaurant, and saw him lead his men off the following day. Fergusson had held my job a year

46

before me; then in 1943 he led a column in Wingate's first Chindit operation, and wrote a book about it. It opened with the words, 'The walls of the room in which I worked in Delhi were covered in maps.' This rang a bell with me. After reading it I said to a friend, 'I thought Fergusson was bright, but this book shows him as totally loyal to Wingate, who he proves to be a walking disaster.' The reply was, 'That shows how bright Fergusson is.'

Our next stop was the Arakan, where the cultivated coastal strip was confined on one side by the sea, and on the other by a steep ridge about 1,500 feet high, which stretched for miles. Beyond the ridge almost impenetrable jungle extended, making the Arakan vitally important. The 5th Indian Division held the coastal strip and on the other side of the ridge the 7th Indian Division was in contact with the Japanese, and beyond them the 31st West African Division was deployed out in the jungle. The West Africans, led by British officers, were entirely at home in the jungle, and fought well. One of them, on leave in Calcutta, was greeted by a black American soldier, whom he closely resembled. The American came away scratching his head, saying, 'That damn nigger can't speak English.'

Having arrived safely, we spent the next day inspecting the 5th Division and then drove over the pass to spend the night at 7th Division headquarters, commanded by Major-General Frank Messervy, an old polo friend. He told us how, when commanding the 7th Armoured Division in the Western Desert at the battle of Knightsbridge, his headquarters had been overrun by German panzers. Expecting capture, he had stripped off his badges of rank and pretended to be a sentry. A suspicious German officer questioned him about his DSO ribbon, given only to officers, but Messervy had explained, 'I was an officer once, but drink was my downfall.' As a private soldier he was less closely guarded than the officers and managed to escape, but then had been transferred back to India, as no longer wanted in theatre.

We spent the evening being briefed by Messervy, but during the night there was gunfire to the north, suggesting that the Japanese had got right round behind us. Clearly the inspection tour would have to be called off, and I was told to get my general out quickly. We made our way back to the pass, but there was some congestion at the foot of it, and while we were halted Zero fighters dive-bombed, albeit to little effect. As soon as the enemy aircraft had departed I found a wounded man who could not move, so I carried him back to his ambulance. He could not explain how he had come to be twenty yards from it.

I saw General Giffard off by plane, but remained behind in case I could be of use. Sleeping at corps headquarters that night I heard more gunfire, this time to the south, and in the morning I was asked to investigate. The Japanese had sent a party to climb over the ridge intending to cut the vital coastal road, but in the dark they had blundered into the corps administrative area, where their unexpected arrival caused havoc and left a few men dead. Instead of pressing ahead and cutting the road, however, they had pulled back into the jungle. No one had pursued them, so I went into the jungle to see if they were still there. I discovered where some of the party had eaten breakfast, and brought back some abandoned Japanese newspapers in case they were of interest to intelligence. Rather than return to corps, I stayed with the troops that night, mainly to calm trigger-happy men firing at shadows. Meanwhile, the main body of invading Japanese had overrun Messervy's headquarters, but this time he had made his escape in a tank. The enemy had taken the foot of the pass, so the 7th Division was surrounded, marking the beginning of what became known as the battle of the Box.

The Corps had at its disposal just one tank regiment, the 25th Dragoons, which was with the 7th Division, except for a dozen tanks with crews in reserve at the Administrative Area. I suggested that I should form a fighting squadron from the reserve tanks and their crews, and was also given a troop of South African scout cars and a company of bloodthirsty Gharwalis for close protection. They were near neighbours of the Gurkhas, and had a reputation for being almost as brave. Having assembled this mixed force, I led it to the top of the pass, which we held with the Japanese at the foot. Meanwhile, to the surprise of the enemy, the 7th Division was supplied by air, and we had a grandstand view of the parachute drop. As the Japanese launched determined attacks night after night we came to be glad of the fierce Gharwalis.

Each morning we netted wireless sets to a new frequency. On the first day an additional, highly suspicious station came up asking for the position of our headquarters, and I replied with a map reference in the Indian Ocean. I then made inquiries as to the rudest word in Japanese.

Stuart light tank: James's would do 60 mph forwards – or backwards.

Mountbatten and Slim take the Japanese surrender in Singapore.

Churchill walks the deck of *HMS Prince of Wales* during the Atlantic Conference August 1941 that established the overarching war aims enshrined in the Atlantic Charter.

I was told, 'Damarey' phonetically, meaning, 'Kindly take yourself elsewhere', a terrible insult. When I used it to my caller the next day he was so humiliated that he never reappeared on the airwaves.

Just half a mile away were some brother officers, now with the 25th Dragoons, but surrounded by the Japanese. They were 'Frinky' Frink, commanding, Hugh Ley, second-in-command, and squadron-leaders Charles Sloan and Tony Johnston, who won a DSO there. On one foray, Tony's tank drove into an open clearing and found some Japanese, who roared with laughter at the joke of being surprised, as they were shot down. Hugh Ley shared his slit trench with Messervy and Brigadier Geoff Evans, who had just served as commandant at the Staff College. Ley's batman, who had been a butler in civilian life, brought them early-morning tea, but the gruff Evans failed to thank him, and was reproved with the words, 'You should remember, sir, that you are a guest in Major Ley's trench.'

The three were to remain together for the next fifteen months on the long road to Rangoon, for Ley became chief staff officer of the division, and when in October 1944 Messervy became their corps commander, Evans took over command of the division.

After a few days of the siege, when the gunners were firing mortars, a shell burst prematurely and took a large chunk out of my right forearm, cutting open the artery. I put my finger on the pressure point at my elbow, and then obtained a tourniquet from the medical officer, so I did not lose too much blood. By sheer good fortune there was a field surgical unit with an operating table in a tent not far away, where my artery was repaired, saving my arm. Taking stock, the sportsman in me realised that it was the right arm that had suffered. 'But that's the wrong one,' I blurted out. The loss of an arm can be an embarrassment. On an official tour with Jack Profumo years later, his private secretary had only a stump, so when we visited the Persian Gulf, where theft entails the loss of a hand, the Arabs wondered what awful crime he had committed.

I was followed on to the operating table by a Japanese prisoner with a severe groin wound. He seemed to be a particularly anxious patient and was believed to have participated in an attack a few days earlier when the 7th Division's advanced dressing station had been overrun. Everyone, staff and patients alike, had been butchered, and although he was suspected of this atrocity he received excellent treatment. Nevertheless that night, in the bed next to mine, he had torn off all his dressings to see whether he had been mutilated. My Japanese companion would soon find himself interrogated by a Japanese-American wearing American uniform. This was an appalling shock to a patriotic Japanese soldier.

After the battle of the Box, the British moved south to reach the Maungdaw to Buthialaming tunnel, another crossing of the Mayu range. A formation of Japanese troops were known to be holed up inside; to winkle them out conventionally would have proved suicidal. Instead 5 Division brought up an anti-aircraft gun and lined it up with the tunnel, so that its shots ricocheted all the way down. Soon a Japanese soldier, not as brave as most, appeared with a white flag. Questioned as to what had happened, he said that the officer had ordered them all to commit hara-kiri. Asked why had he not obeyed, he said he had not heard the order.

In Delhi, news of my wound inspired Dmitri Zvegintzov, ever the humourist, to celebrate in verse:

Planner James, 3rd Carabiniers,
Hadn't heard a shot for years.
Planning simply drove him barmy:
'Damn it all I joined the army
With some vague idea of fighting;
Found the Gunners unexciting;
So I joined, the world the see
HM's Carbs, or 3rd DG.'

And so James made a cunning plan,
Which took him to the Arakan.
And there, without a word of thanks
He just took over all the tanks.
Down the hill the tanks would rumble,
Down in heaps the Japs would tumble.

Causing fearful Nippon losses,
Earning deathless fame and crosses.
So fought James, and only stopping
When the beer supply was dropping.

And then, despite all others' claim,
To seize it all was James's aim.
This caused the Gunners some alarm.
And so, not wishing too much harm,
They winged our James in his right arm.
The moral, so it would appear,
Is, don't take other people's beer.

My consolation was that one of my tanks became the first to break through the Japanese lines to relieve the Box. The wound was sufficiently severe to require immediate evacuation and the day after my operation I travelled many miles by ambulance over bumpy roads to Comilla Hospital, en route for Calcutta. But the Comilla surgeon wanted to try his hand at a skin graft, so for the next month I lay in a plaster cast with my arm tied to my stomach. The objective was to cover the gaping wound in my arm with skin from my abdomen, thereby making a fearful mess of both. This somewhat primitive procedure was intensely time-consuming, and left part of me resembling a patchwork quilt, but it had the merit of avoiding the deadly infection associated with open wounds and left me with the use of one arm.

Naturally, as this was in Burma, there were no amenities in the hospital, except for the library, which consisted of five tattered paperbacks, which I read several times. The only book I had with me in my kitbag was Clausewitz's *Principles of War*. Finally, after a month, the surgeon admitted defeat, and allowed me to fly to Calcutta Hospital, where I had friends and comforts, and above all a team of skin-graft specialists trained by Sir Archie McIndoe at the famous burns unit at East Grinstead. A fellow patient, a pilot, was having all the skin on his back replaced. I was offered a cosmetic job or a quick fix. I chose the quick fix.

While I was in hospital the Chindit airborne operation took place, and part of Brigadier Calvert's brigade was flown in by glider to construct an airstrip. General Slim came to watch the glider take off. Seeing some of his favourite Gurkhas, he went over to a party sitting patiently in a glider and asked them how they reckoned it would fly, since it had no engine. 'No doubt some Sahib will make an arrangement,' was the reply. In Italy one of these Gurkhas had returned from night patrol chuckling. He reported that he had discovered three

Germans sleeping under blankets, so had cut off the heads of the outer two and swapped them round. The amusement lay in contemplating the surprise of the survivor when he woke in the morning.

Despite the assurances we had received, the task of tugging two gliders behind each Dakota proved extremely difficult, and many had to be released halfway. Peter Fleming, still in charge of deception, thumbed a lift, and when his glider was cast off over Japanese territory, he used his experience as an explorer to lead his party safely out, and then wrote an amusing account of the episode. Hearing of this, Mountbatten chuckled that his staff officers were showing a keen interest in the war, but some spoilsport pointed out the danger of capture, and an order was issued forbidding those with a knowledge of future operations from risking capture. The directive was principally intended as a rebuke to Fleming and myself, although I was unaware of it at the time.

Upon my release from hospital in early April 1944 I reported to 14th Army Headquarters and learned that Orde Wingate had just been killed. He had been flying to a meeting when his aircraft had landed at an American airfield to refuel. His pilot reported the weather ahead made it impossible to fly on, so Wingate turned to some American pilots and said, "My British pilot is too yellow to fly me on. Will one of you do it?" His own pilot said that if he felt like that about it he would fly him, but it would be certain death, and so it proved. In nil visibility their plane flew into the side of a mountain and all aboard perished.

The Chindits had been ordered by 14th Army to move north but did not seem to be making much progress, so I was instructed to investigate. Finding them still completely committed to the Wingate plan to be carried out by Fergusson's brigade, I suggested that I should fly in to discuss it with him. This was approved and that same afternoon I arrived to find his brigade exhausted after nearly three months behind enemy lines. Fergusson was willing to make a last effort to capture Indaw, after which the plan called for his men to be replaced with a fresh division. I explained that the last operational division had just been committed against a threatened Japanese invasion of India, so if he captured Indaw, he would have to garrison it himself, which was clearly impossible. I flew back that evening, and the Wingate plan was abandoned. Fergusson's brigade was flown out, and Master's and Calvert's brigades moved north.

Meanwhile, I returned to 14th Army Headquarters, my mission accomplished, but was met with long faces. I had disobeyed an order, Mountbatten's ban on risky missions, of which I was completely unaware. It was obvious I was totally unwanted. My attachment to 14th Army Headquarters now ended almost before it had begun and I was to return to South-East Asia Command Headquarters. Thus it was that I dined in the opulent luxury of the 300 Club in Calcutta precisely one night after a scratch supper behind the Japanese lines. The contrast could hardly have been greater. One moment I was eating out of a tin, under risk of fire from Japanese snipers, and the next I was being served the best cuisine in the subcontinent by a retinue of turbaned waiters.

By this time Mountbatten's headquarters had moved to Ceylon, and the planning staff had changed. I had been promoted lieutenant-colonel, and the senior army planner. In that role I was mainly preoccupied with future plans for 14th Army recovery, but I also had to deal with the Americans. On General Stilwell's front an American Ranger force had captured an airstrip close to Myitkyina, and was holding the perimeter, but the Chinese troops on the Ledo road were still far off. It was decided to send an Indian division there to help and I flew to Ledo to discuss arrangements with General Pick, Stilwell's chief of administration, and Brigadier George Still of the 14th Army. We were expecting a lengthy discussion, but the US Army attitude was far more relaxed than the cheeseparing British. Pick said he would take anything we offered, noting that, 'Stilwell has a bad tooth, so a dentist would certainly be welcome.'

We were able to finish our discussions before lunch, so Still asked what I wanted to do that afternoon. When I said I would like to go to Myitkyina, he replied that it was a court-martial offence: the idea was dropped. I flew in the cockpit of a C-47, however, and the pilot expressed surprise at my knowledge of the country, gained from long study of the map. We landed stores at the airstrip where the perimeter was held, but no more. The next day Still asked me where I had been, and when I told him he replied, 'I wish I'd come too.'

When the Chindits arrived at the Myitkyina airstrip, they had been too weak and exhausted to assault the strong Japanese garrison of Myitkyina, but the Indian division that replaced them captured the town and the Japanese fled south.

6

Kandy

Sitting close to Ceylon's geographical centre at an altitude of almost five thousand feet, Kandy enjoys a commanding position on the banks of the island's longest river and an enviable climate. Close by stands the Dalada Maligawa, the Temple of the Sacred Tooth of the Buddha. Brought to Sri Lanka in the fourth century AD, the relic was the traditional symbol of sovereignty for the island's Sinhalese kings. I wondered how long it would be before the tooth ended up on the Supreme Commander's mantelpiece. He had had little hesitation in commandeering the Royal Pavilion as his seat.

South-East Asia Command Headquarters was now an integrated Anglo-American organisation with General Albert C. Wedemeyer as Chief-of-Staff. Like Stilwell, he was a confirmed anglophobe. Although the United States had been drawn into the war as our ally, there were plenty of isolationists who were opposed to risking American lives in the cause of restoring French, Dutch and British colonies across the Far East. As Wedemeyer had no hesitation in explaining, American logistical support would be available only for operations that furthered their strategy in China. This put the writing on the wall for Operation Dracula, the combined air and amphibious assault on Rangoon, to which we had devoted so many late nights.

My American opposite number was Lieutenant-Colonel Dean Rusk, later President John F. Kennedy's Secretary of State. A former Rhodes scholar, he had served with the 3rd Infantry Division before secondment to the Military Intelligence Service. It was his habit to keep in a locked drawer a ruled pad with a list of problems on it. In those days the list extended to a couple of dozen items. By the time he reached the office of Secretary of State in 1961 it had reached several hundred. Although we got on well, Rusk remained the soul of discretion. His clueless major, however, used to attend the US personnel-only briefings, and then come and blurt out everything he had heard to us. Unofficially, the American policy was to keep the British bogged down in Burma, so that we would not recapture Malaya, regain our colonial territory and exercise the economic strength associated with it. Why should the Americans exert themselves to put Britain back into the international rubber market?

The Army Director of Plans was Brigadier Brian Kimmins, the same man who had been the strict and terrifying adjutant at the RMA Woolwich, now perfectly charming, and who became a good friend. While he was away, as when attending the Cairo Conference, I became acting Director of Plans.

When it was my turn to be taken out to lunch by Mountbatten I felt more embarrassed than impressed by the huge car flying all the Allied flags, and the constant references to 'my sister, the Queen of Sweden'. Self-aggrandisement seemed to be the fuel he ran on, a curious combination of approval-seeking and showing off antithetic to the relaxed self-deprecation of army culture. On form he could rouse the troops, but his vanities and transparent deceptions rarely failed to irritate the officers upon whom he relied for success.

If Mountbatten's confidence in his own ability rarely wavered, I swiftly learned the necessity of caution. For all his charm and acuteness, his attitude to the truth tended to be flexible, coloured as much by wish as reality; before proceeding one learned to double-check any facts imparted by the supremo. He gave instructions that if any signal from the Chiefs of Staff in London arrived during the night, it was to be brought to him whatever the hour. He would then dictate an immediate answer, and proudly produce it to the Directors of Plans the next morning. They would point out the errors in his reply, so he would order its retraction. He was not to know that the signal had never been sent on our instructions.

Years later, when Mrs Gandhi, from political spite, imprisoned Ayesha Jaipur, her friends in London organised a protest. But when Mountbatten, who was trustee to the Jaipur children, was invited to support it he declined because of 'my royal connections'. Only those who did not know him well were surprised.

The most senior officers had their own messes in which to reside and dine, in which they could talk confidentially. General Giffard invited me to live in his mess, so that I could tell him the latest developments over dinner, thus sparing me the horrors of the Anglo–American officers' mess, where differing habits and timing of meals and drink had led to mutual antipathy.

Soon we were hard at work on alternative plans for the recapture of Burma before the 1945 monsoon, and the one selected emphasised the success of the medium tank and massive air supply, both of which I had recently experienced at first hand. In August a conference was called, attended by all the generals, Stilwell included, to approve the final plan. Stilwell surprised everyone by announcing that he had an alternative plan, which he then described as, 'Brits hold the Japs on the Chindwin, while I run around left end', a phrase apparently used in American football. If his plan had been adopted, the Japanese would have remained in Rangoon, which is what the Americans wanted. Had the plan been serious, Dean Rusk should have put it forward at an earlier stage, but it was merely Stilwell expressing his usual contempt for British military efforts. Reverting to the scheme proposed General Philip Christison, commanding the corps in the Arakan, objected that he could not possibly capture Akyab by February, as required. Unimpressed, Mountbatten replied, 'Let my planners have a look at it.'

My team worked all night to produce a plan for a massive air strike, followed by a seaborne assault, which Christison accepted. In the event, the Japanese abandoned Akyab without fighting, so the operation was transferred to a site further south at Kyaukpyu, which was strongly held by the Japanese. Part of the bombardment force was the battleship *Queen Elizabeth*, which had not fired its fifteen-inch guns in anger since the Dardarnelles in 1915. General Christison was on the bridge. The first salvo fell beyond the target into a swamp, sending up flights of duck. Christison called out, 'Duck', but the Admiral reproved him, 'In the Royal Navy we never duck.' The remaining salvoes were on target, and the operation proved a success.

Next we had to consider Malaya. The Chiefs of Staff in London asked for plans, so I drafted a reply for Mountbatten, 'I have not sufficient intelligence to plan the operation.' The Directors of Plans approved this, and were about to take it in to Mountbatten, when I confessed to the double meaning. The signal was hurriedly redrafted.

As we prepared for the retaking of Malaya it became clear that a refuelling airstrip for fighters would be needed halfway between

Rangoon and Malaya. I found on the map the island of Phuket, which turned out to be entirely suitable, so I named it Operation ROGER. This news duly reached London where the name delighted the Prime Minister; when someone objected that a codename should have no connection with the real name, Winston had sent for the list of unallocated codenames and picked out one or two with a similar meaning. Thus the capture and development of Phuket remained Operation Roger. The somewhat primitive airstrip has now grown into an international airport, and the name is now pronounced slightly differently.

In November 1944 General Giffard was replaced by General Oliver Leese. Giffard, widely known as the worst-dressed general in the army for his ill-fitting tunics and creased trousers, was put in charge of a War Office committee to consider post-war army attire. I was reminded of Admiral Fisher's prediction, 'One day we shall lose the empire because it was Buggin's turn.'

Leese had drunk deep of Montgomery's philosophy, but lacked his master's flair. A man of limited modesty, he wanted to make an immediate impression, so what better than sacking Bill Slim? After all, he was a defensive general. But Slim had the extraordinary right of direct communication with Churchill bypassing the chain of command, and very soon Mountbatten received a message from the Prime Minister demanding, "What's all this about sacking my wonderful General Slim?" Sensing Churchill's interest, Mountbatten swiftly came about, and Slim stayed, eventually gazetted Field Marshal Viscount Slim of Burma, while Leese ended up as General Sir Oliver.

I had not been particularly keen to serve under Leese. I had also tired of planning, and wanted to see action in Germany. After seven years of service overseas, I was entitled to a posting home. I was offered the job of instructor at the Staff College, Camberley, which I refused, but my old Delhi friend, the poet Zvegintzov accepted. Although a White Russian, he got on well with the military staff at the Russian Embassy, who visited Camberley frequently. But the end of the war in Europe was also the end of Glasnost. His embassy friends were replaced by hard-faced men who would have nothing to do with him.

By a fortunate coincidence, Mountbatten's private plane was going to England to bring out his wife, Edwina. Thus General Playfair and I were offered passages home, at speed and in conditions of unaccustomed comfort. Stopping overnight at Naples, we were put up at General Sir Harold Alexander's villa in his absence. When we came to sign the guest-book in the morning the signatures above ours proved to be those of Winston Churchill and Anthony Eden; I reflected how lucky Alexander was to get our three illustrious names on the same page.

As for Mountbatten, I had left him dreaming of advancement, both military and political. It was clear that he remained fixed upon India as the place in which he might rule as a monarch, and secure a more prominent place in history as the last British viceroy. What he was unable to foresee, though the dangers were apparent to those around him, was that in place of glory would fall responsibility for the over-hasty partition of India that led to slaughter, and embarrassment at his wife Edwina's intimacy with the Congress leader, Jawaharlal Nehru.

7

MO5

Back in England after seven eventful years in the Far East, I found there was no shortage of unemployed Royal Armoured Corps officers, so getting to Germany was not going to be easy. One needed to be applied for personally, so I started to pull strings. It was not until February 1945 that I was requested as a brigade major, but by that time I was already in a job.

On arrival home in December 1944 I had called on my former opposite number as planner in the War Office to compare notes. He told me that he was just off to the Yalta Conference in the Crimea. One of the aircraft carrying senior Cabinet Office personnel lost its way in poor weather on the flight to Malta and crashed in the Mediterranean. All the crew and passengers were killed, and suddenly, an experienced grade-one planner was required in a hurry. I was all too available, and was put straight to work in a department of the War Office designated MO5.

Although my office was in the main building, the Joint Planning Staff (JPS) met in the Cabinet War Rooms below George Street where I met my naval counterpart, Captain 'Ruggy' MacIntosh, later Black Rod in the House of Lords. He was not the fastest torpedo in the navy, so I worked with his subordinate, Commander Alan Noble. When we had reached the final draft of a paper we would show it to Ruggy, knowing that if he understood it, everyone else would too. The JPS consisted of a Strategic Planning Section, Future Plans Section and an Executive Planning Sector, where I worked.

There was one improvement I sought to initiate immediately. Mountbatten's tactic was to inflate his requests by half on the grounds that London would cut whatever was requested. My attempt to introduce some honesty into the system was not successful, however.

59

The Cabinet War Rooms, to which I was frequently summoned to give briefings, attend meetings and amend plans, occupied the fortified basement of the steel-framed Office of Works building in Storey's Gate opposite St James's Park, the strongest structure in Whitehall. Known simply as 'George Street' or 'Storey's Gate', it was protected by a raft of concrete several feet thick strengthened with tram rails and had been designed to resist a direct hit, an engineering calculation fortunately never put to the test.

Work had started in June 1938, the War Room becoming operational on 27 August 1939, just a week before the declaration of war following the German invasion of Poland. Fifty feet below ground, it was designed to house and sleep a permanent staff of 270, with additional offices for regular visitors such as my own team, in some 150 rooms. A sub-basement with low ceilings housed cramped dormitories crammed with bunk beds. The complex was huge, with six acres of floor space and a mile of corridors, but only chemical lavatories. While hardly comfortable the atmosphere was purposeful; few of the visitors escorted in by the Royal Marine guards were left in any doubt that this was the hub of the war effort and centre of decision-making.

Within, the bunker was permanently lit, making it impossible to tell whether it was day or night when you looked at your watch. Winston's bedroom was not close enough to our office to hear him snoring, so the best test was to see whether what we had prepared made any sense when typed up the next day. That composed at 4 p.m. was notably better than the 4 a.m. version. The Premier's sleeping habits were in any event an unreliable guide, as he was as likely to take an afternoon siesta as he was to keep the Chiefs-of-Staff up most of the night, often with us in attendance. (More frequently, though, he worked and slept immediately above us in the six first-floor rooms of the Number 10 Annexe, the windows barred with steel shutters during the bombing.)

Periodically the Prime Minister would disappear into his private lavatory, which otherwise remained securely locked. And there he would remain for a considerable time, giving rise among the secretaries to a tender concern about his insides. It was a closely guarded secret that behind the door, with its 'Occupied/Vacant' sign, the PM was talking over an encrypted transatlantic radio link to the President of the United States. An early computer, located in an annexe basement of Selfridges department store in Oxford Street, was required to scramble speech

Cabinet Room in the Cabinet War Rooms bunker. Meetings continued round the clock.

Mountbatten and two close friends: Edwina and Nehru were more than friendly.

securely on this, the first 'hot line'. The highly classified system was codenamed SIGSALY, the London terminal being X-RAY.

At the figurative centre of the George Street complex was the Cabinet Room, in which a square had been formed of trestle tables covered in baize, with a narrow gap to allow members of the secretariat into the centre to take notes. Around the outside facing in would sit members of the War Cabinet and Chiefs-of-Staff. Whatever the hour at which I passed through the sandbagged and securely guarded entrance to the bunker a meeting was likely to be in progress in the Cabinet Room. From it issued a stream of demands for information, some of which it was our task as planners to answer.

Next to the Prime Minister's bedroom was the Map Room, from which he had broadcast to the nation during the dark days of 1940, and where he still met heads of state and military leaders. The walls were covered with large-scale maps of Britain, the Atlantic and Far Eastern theatres of war, bearing notes of force deployments and convoys. These were kept constantly updated with the latest information. When my eightieth birthday party was celebrated in the War Rooms in September 1993 the maps remained as they had been on the last day of the war – and my name appeared on the duty roster posted outside Winston's bedroom.

An essential component of planning is access to the best intelligence, and my principal source of processed intelligence was Bill Cavendish-Bentinck, the immensely successful Chairman of the Joint Intelligence Committee (JIC) who was also the Foreign Office Adviser to the Director of Plans. I was not told that he was of ambassadorial rank (and was soon to be appointed British Ambassador in Warsaw), and always found him very helpful and never stuffy. This was unusual among diplomats of the period. Bill had succeeded Ralph Stevenson as Chairman at the JIC and had the personality to co-ordinate all Britain's intelligence activities. It was an immense task, but it was one he fulfilled with rare skill and tact. He was admired by all the directors of intelligence, perhaps with the exception of Admiral John Godfrey at the Admiralty, who rightly suspected that Cavendish-Bentinck was arranging his removal from his post because he was uncooperative and disruptive. Godfrey was transferred to the Indian Navy in 1943, minus the anticipated knighthood.

In 1947, when Cavendish-Bentinck became embroiled in a messy divorce, he was obliged to resign from the Foreign Service. The Labour

Foreign Secretary, Ernest Bevin, who liked him immensely, said, 'I could have saved you had your name been Smith.'

I soon learned that Churchill had a habit of bombarding the Chiefs-of-Staff with queries and suggestions, which they then passed to the Directors of Plans, who in turn filtered them to whichever of the three teams was concerned. The reply would return by the same route. One day in February I found in my in-tray just such a query: 'In view of the impending defeat of Germany, pray let me know the effect of reducing dry cargo shipping for the forces by: a) 25 per cent; b) 50 per cent. W.S.C.'

Having researched the issue I found that there was two months' stock of ammunition in Italy and a further month's supply on the way. Our report showed that a 25 per cent cut was acceptable, but 50 per cent would bring severe difficulties. Characteristically, the Prime Minister imposed the 50 per cent cut.

Soon afterwards, we had to allocate conflicting demands for personnel shipping upon the defeat of Germany. Chief among the considerations were:

1. A large airfield construction group to Okinawa. The Prime Minister was set on this, to let Japan know what it was like to be the target of Bomber Command.
2. The invasion of Malaya, bearing in mind that Mountbatten always asked for 50 per cent more than he needed.
3. Redeployment. The replacement from Europe of troops who had been too long in Burma.

Before long, I received a cable from Washington: 'Top Secret, CIGS copy. The Combined Chiefs of Staff have approved the plan for personnel shipping.' I put this in my pocket and walked over the road to QMG House to show it to the Director of Movement, General Williams, but when I got back to my office it had disappeared. The Chief of the Imperial General Staff, however, seemed undisturbed at this appalling breach of security.

At that time the War Office required the Military Operations branches to provide a colonel to be on duty every night, ready to react to emergencies. It happened to be my turn when the BBC nine o'clock news announced that General Montgomery was meeting German representatives to discuss an armistice, though Monty had not troubled to inform the War Office. As word spread the CIGS, the Director of Military Operations and most of the top brass homed in on the War Office – and I had a peaceful night.

During the summer a committee from India arrived, established to settle the post-war shape of the Indian Army. It was composed of brigadiers, and headed by a major-general, and among the team was one Brigadier Enoch Powell. As soon as I heard this I felt sorry for the major-general, but the war ended too soon, and Enoch failed in his plan to achieve that rank. On leaving the army he joined the Conservative Research Department and when I saw another member of his team, I warned him, 'You should watch that boy Enoch: one day he will be Prime Minister.' 'No,' came the reply. 'To become Prime Minister you must be popular with your colleagues.' Later Enoch married the vivacious Pamela and joined the human race.

When the General Election of 1945 was called, I would have liked to have stood for Parliament, but I felt that the job I was doing was so important that I could not be spared. My colleague Alan Noble, however, had no such inhibitions when he was offered the safe seat of Chelsea.

Our last wartime job on the Joint Planning Staff was to despatch an Airfield Construction Group to Okinawa to build airfields for Bomber Command in anticipation of operations against Japan in 1946. It arrived just as the Japanese surrendered, and was usefully diverted to Hong Kong.

On the day of the Japanese surrender I went to my Director of Plans with the completed scheme for the formation and training in Canada of a Commonwealth Corps, before taking part in the invasion of Japan in the spring of 1947. He told me that I knew exactly where to put it.

It was the policy of the European Allies, but not of the United States, that pre-war colonies in Asia should be reoccupied. At the defeat of Japan, the boundaries of South-East Asia Command were extended to include the whole of Java and French Indo-China (now Vietnam) up to the sixteenth parallel of latitude. Responsibility north of the line went to the chairman of the Chinese national government, Generalissimo Chiang Kai-Shek, who made little effort to restore to the French their territory, but allowed Ho Chi Minh to form an administration. In the southern zone, Major-General Douglas Gracey brought in his 20th

Indian Division, which suppressed disturbances and duly handed over to the French at the end of the year.

In Java, Lieutenant General Sir Philip Christison with his Fifteenth Corps from the Arakan did not enjoy the same success. He settled in the city of Batavia, which he failed to subdue. His first priority was the rescue of prisoners of war, including many civilians, in a hostile atmosphere. There could be no question of imposing his will on the vast territory of Java.

When challenged about the position there, Mountbatten, now in Singapore, was curiously evasive. Accordingly, in December 1945, I was sent out, with the title of 'Personal Representative of the CIGS' to report on the situation. What I found in Java was truly extraordinary, for the Dutch forces were being prevented from engaging the Indonesian insurgents by the British, who were so enthusiastic about pursuing this policy that they had armed the remnants of the Japanese Army to hold off the rebels. Christison, it emerged, had taken a dislike to the Dutch, believing they would treat all Javans as hostile; he had thus confined them to barracks and rearmed the Japanese instead. This did little to improve the prestige of the former colonial rulers among those of the population who favoured a return to Dutch rule and prosperity.

Mountbatten went along with this, but as it was completely at variance with British policy, he kept London in the dark. Since he was willing to take credit for Gracie's success in South Indo-China, he cannot have been implementing American policy in Java intentionally. Rather, I believe, it came from his wish to leave it to the commander on the spot, whether competent or otherwise. Following my report to the CIGS the Dutch were, from the beginning of 1946, permitted to try to recover their colony; but it was too late. After several years they would be obliged to concede failure. The French also failed to re-establish control of South Vietnam, but the British after fourteen years' resourceful campaigning, did manage to defeat the communist insurgency in Malaya. So the job could be done.

Analysis of the situation in Java produced valuable lessons that contributed to the subsequent success of the Malay campaign. Laurens van der Post, who had been a prisoner in Java, told me of the 'singing trees' in every village which had been fitted with loudspeakers broadcasting anti-European propaganda by the Japanese, stirring up the insurgency in the first place. While a prisoner of war Laurens had organised a camp university and even a camp farm, greatly raising the morale of his comrades. After liberation he had remained in Java and on 15th September 1945 had been invited aboard HMS *Cumberland* to witness Admiral William Patterson receive the formal surrender of the Japanese. He would later mediate between the Dutch and the Indonesian nationalists, an extraordinary saga, although one he did not record until half a century later in *The Admiral's Baby*.

On my way to the airfield to fly back to Singapore, my Jeep driver was shot in the arm by an Indonesian sniper, leaving me to arrive back in Singapore covered in his blood. Having changed and written my report, I was invited by Mountbatten to a cosy dinner. He asked to see the report. I had, he informed me, completely misunderstood the position and he would do me the honour of rewriting it. His version turned out to be a complete travesty, amounting to a cover-up; I was so angry that I tore it up in the car on my way back to Raffles Hotel.

8

Post-war Army Service

In January 1946 I married Nuala McArevey, a lovely Irish actress just making a name for herself on the London stage.

Nuala soon received a taste of the discomforts of army life when I was briefly appointed an instructor at the School of Combined Operations near Bideford, and we found a furnished cottage at Bucks Mills, the next village to Clovelly. There was no electricity, so we were lit and cooked by oil, and I carried water in from an outside pump. Our lavatory was a shed with a straight drop into the village stream.

The local villagers were all named Braund, said to be descended from survivors of the Spanish Armada, so our daily help was therefore called 'Mrs Walter'. Rationing was still in force, but I was allowed petrol coupons to drive to work in my drop-head Railton; instead I rode to work on a motorcycle. The only trouble with this economy was that it proved the wettest summer on record.

Among the more memorable events during my posting to Devon was the occasion when the instructors took a landing craft to Normandy, with the object of studying the D-Day landings. When we returned we each had a case of brandy aboard, on which duty was payable. This was high on a three-star bottle, but when the customs officer saw my case labelled 'Grand Fine Champagne' he charged me champagne duty, which was much lower.

In the autumn I managed to escape my posting, and we returned to London, where I was appointed to the Joint Administrative Planning Staff under Major-General Fielding. He was a keen racing man who liked to be able to leave everything to his subordinates, so he eyed me with a gloomy stare for two months until he found he could trust me.

Planning the British contribution to the Berlin Airlift, I learned for the first time of dehydrated potatoes, the lightest form of nourishment.

Given the German obsession with sausage this would, we reckoned, be the opportunity to introduce Berliners to the delights of the English delicacy, bangers and mash. The suggestion was met with bemusement by German quartermasters reared on sauerkaut.

One problem facing the Planning Staff concerned Palestine, which had been a British responsibility since the 1919 Treaty of Versailles. It was Britain's thankless responsibility to protect a Jewish homeland in a country that had been Arab for many centuries. Mass emigration from Europe at the end of the war had exacerbated a difficult situation, leaving us with the choice of repelling an Arab invasion or keeping out the immigrants. We chose the latter course, and thereby precipitated an urban guerrilla war by Jewish extremists.

Clearly army reinforcements were required, but none were available, so the Foreign Secretary, Ernest Bevin, devised a cunning scheme. He would threaten to abandon Palestine, leaving the Arabs to drive the Jews into the sea, a situation that would be wholly unacceptable to the powerful Jewish lobby in the United States, thereby forcing America to come to Britain's assistance. With the USA involved in Palestine, Britain's burden could be shared and the Arabs would not dare attack.

The Chiefs of Staff were asked how long it would take for Palestine to be evacuated, and the question was put to my team. As there was no mention of haste, I decided to plan for a dignified withdrawal, taking all our military equipment and stores. The key consideration was the freight capacity at the port of Haifa, so we needed to know the precise amount of materiel to be shifted. Unfortunately, the War Office could account only for the ammunition, so when I suggested a working factor of two tonnes per man, nobody objected, and this was calculated to take up the port's full capacity for six months. To this figure we added two months for preparation and the positioning of shipping, plus a further month to cover contingencies.

Accordingly, the Chiefs of Staff reported that a British withdrawal would take nine months, and the appropriate orders were given, the Americans not having fallen for Bevin's plan to force them to come to our assistance. In the event the entire operation took only eight months, during which time the Arabs were held off and the Jews given sufficient time to prepare their defences. The subsequent war provided the Jews with a great victory over the Arabs, and the State of Israel came into existence.

Had I decided to plan to evacuate Palestine as swiftly as possible, we could have used the railway to Egypt to move stores there, to be shipped home later. In that case, the Jews would not have had time to arm themselves and the Arabs would have won. There would thus have been no State of Israel.

In 1948 an appreciation of Soviet capabilities in the event of war had been required. The Joint Intelligence Committee (JIC) declined the task because it was so dependent upon logistics, but I volunteered my team to undertake it. Investigating Russian logistics I discovered that they were excellent at running a line of communication by rail. If a bridge was destroyed, instead of appealing for help from Moscow, they turned out the local population to fell trees and to build a wooden bridge, which appeared in double-quick time. They were less effective with road traffic. A convoy lorry route would soon spawn local fairs with dancing bears and vodka dens, which distracted the drivers somewhat.

Our first draft of the situation on the German front, anticipating a dash to the Channel, was seen by Field-Marshal Montgomery as CIGS. This was too pessimistic, he told me, wagging his finger, albeit with the hint of a smile. So in our final paper the Russians were stopped at the Rhine. This was approved by the British Chiefs of Staff, and I accompanied the Directors of Plans to Washington DC to present it to the Pentagon. The Americans accepted the analysis, and since Europe supposedly had been proved to be defensible, the United States joined the North Atlantic Treaty.

In 1947 Nuala and I went with David and Diana Strathcarron on a short visit to Paris in David's car. We stayed in the cheapest hotel we could discover, the Royal Fromentin in Montmartre. It was spotlessly clean, but there was a lot of noise from clients coming and going throughout the night. We were given seats for the collections of Jacques Fath and Dior, but eyebrows were raised when we gave our address. What were Milord and Milady doing in a brothel? Fath was showing the *New Look*, dresses with tight waists and full calf-length skirts, a revolution after the economies of war time. In England, Nuala had her beaver coat lengthened and remodelled, and was enchanted to be stopped and accused of smuggling a new coat the next time she passed through customs.

In May of 1948 Nuala gave birth to our first son, Julian, an affectionate child destined to become a pioneer of the personal computer revolution and a great traveller. For a decade readers of the *Financial Times* would be entertained by his monthly essays from exotic destinations. But all of that was unimaginable as I looked at the pink creature in my wife's arms, for austerity had survived wartime and showed little sign of retreat.

Nuala persuaded me to buy a house in London, so that however much we had to serve overseas, there would always be a home to come back to. Thus we bought 16 Chapel Street, off Belgrave Square, and thereafter she never left her London home except for holidays.

In 1949 it was time for me to return to regimental duty, so I rejoined the regiment at Tidworth and brought my hunter, Weedon, with me. Whereas I had enjoyed four horses before the war at nil outlay, it now cost me the equivalent of a subaltern's pay to keep one.

After twelve months of regimental duty the War Office sent me on a six-month course at the Joint Services Staff College to learn about Joint planning. As this was precisely the work I had undertaken for four and a half years during and after the war, I did not find any of it particularly taxing, but I was amused when the final exercise was to plan the capture of the Andaman Islands.

Having completed the course, I was posted to run the discipline branch of the War Office, where I was to stay for three and a half years. Instead of 'action this day', to which I had become so accustomed, our work revolved around the use of official files. I once wrote to a correspondent, 'Dear Madam, Thank you for your letter. I had to indent on Central Registry to obtain your file, who took it from the branch that was dealing with it. I then drafted this letter, which went for typing and my signature, before the file could be returned to the branch that had been dealing with it. So, every time you write to enquire how your case is progressing, a delay of about a fortnight ensues.' Happily she did not write to thank me.

For Parliamentary Questions and similar inquiries, we used priority files. For example, when a Guards officer fainted on the Queen's Birthday Parade, having enjoyed too good a party the previous evening, the newspapers reported that he had been given twenty-eight days confined to barracks. Inevitably there was a Parliamentary Question about the legality of such a punishment for an officer, and the reply I drafted confirmed that it was not a disciplinary award, but friendly advice from the commanding officer to stay in barracks for a bit. A colour sergeant was heard to say, 'Friendly advice? You could hear the colonel on the other side of the barrack square!''

A sergeant serving in Egypt murdered his wife in order to marry his Egyptian mistress. He was convicted by court martial of murder and sentenced to death. It was my job to brief the Secretary of State on whether he should confirm the sentence. I sent the case to the Home Office, asking what advice they would give to the Home Secretary if it came under their jurisdiction. Back came a conclusive case for confirming the sentence. If you give a minister the slightest hint for clemency, he will seize it. One of the arguments against the death penalty is that it gives the Home Secretary sleepless nights. Any sleepless nights are had by the Home Office officials.

The sentence duly confirmed, I negotiated his fee with the hangman, Albert Pierrepoint, and sent a staff captain to see him through Heathrow. He travelled under a different name and insisted that the rope went out by diplomatic bag. He did a good job and everyone was satisfied, except perhaps the sergeant. By the time he resigned in 1956 (after a disagreement over fees) Pierrepoint, the third member of his family to hold the office of Chief Executioner, had dispatched 433 men and seventeen women, including some 200 Nazis following the Nuremburg Trials, and William Joyce, 'Lord Haw-Haw'. Having explained to me the difference between the Long Drop, Short Drop, the Standard Drop and a Suspension Hanging (he favoured the first) Pierrepoint confessed that he was opposed to capital punishment. He was none the less its most efficient exponent: in one execution only seven seconds elapsed from the prisoner leaving his cell to death occurring.

During the Korean War, Fusilier Lyden was on night sentry duty at a forward outpost when an enemy party silently approached. Instead of raising the alarm he surrendered, causing his comrades to be overrun. Some were killed. After a few years he was released from prison camp. His regiment, the Northumberland Fusiliers, who carried the proud title of the Fighting Fifth, wanted him court-martialled to avenge his comrades. I foresaw difficulties, as tender-hearted members of the public, not understanding the appalling nature of the offence, would think he had suffered enough. So I put the case to the Secretary of State, Anthony Head, who approved prosecution. I suggested that the Prime Minister should be informed, and he too gave his agreement.

Lyden was duly convicted by court-martial of cowardice in the face of the enemy, and sentenced to be discharged with ignominy and to serve six months' imprisonment. The *Daily Mail* published a sob story, urging its readers to complain to the Confirming Officer, Lieutenant-General Geoff Evans, he of the slit trench in the battle of the Box.

Until the court martial proceedings were confirmed, the case remained *sub judice*, so I moved swiftly into action. Before noon the Attorney General had taken out a writ for contempt of court against the paper's editor. Later on, the Lord Chief Justice imposed a heavy fine, remarking that he would have preferred to imprison the proprietor, Lord Rothermere.

Back at Downing Street, Churchill had read his *Daily Mail*, and demanded to know who the bloody fool was who had authorised the prosecution, but the name of the culprit was not Allason but his own. I can imagine Jock Colville, his private secretary, saying, 'Ah, as a matter of fact, Prime Minister, you may have forgotten that you approved this document.' The Confirming Officer was given a hint that the Prime Minister had changed his mind, so Lyden escaped imprisonment. To this day, ministers deny influencing courts-martial.

The previous government of Clement Attlee had entrusted supervision of overstaffing at the War Office to Organisation & Methods (O&M) branch, a formation tasked to impose efficiency upon the military machine. They invariably gave a fortnight's warning of their inspection, which allowed an overstaffed branch time to accumulate a huge collection of files in the in-tray, and arrange for a stream of telephone calls. O&M would apologise for interrupting such a busy staff, and depart satisfied. When our time came my branch had no need for such subterfuges.

After the Tory victory in 1951, Churchill ordered a 10 per cent cut in all Whitehall staff, whatever difficulties it might cause. I immediately put in for an additional staff officer on the ground of increased workload, so my branch suffered no cut. But the branch down the corridor suffered a 20 per cent cut with impunity. The army side of the king's funeral, for which they were responsible, and the Coronation both passed off without a hitch. Indeed the whole of Whitehall survived the cut with no obvious loss of efficiency.

That year I took Nuala on her first skiing holiday. We went to Murren in Switzerland's Bernese Oberland, where we stayed at the

Palace Hotel. Other guests included Arnie Lunn, his wife Mabel and her cousin, Field-Marshal Montgomery. No longer the fierce commander who had dismissed my appreciation of Soviet capabilities so imperiously, he had metamorphosed into a charming if undeniably senior figure, albeit unwavering in his views on military matters.

The first morning I took Nuala to the nursery slopes, to teach her the new French system of keeping the skis parallel, running down and then sideslipping to a stop. In the afternoon I left her to practise while I went off to do some serious skiing. Arnie Lunn found her and asked her to do the snowplough or stem turn, then spent the afternoon teaching it to her. Thereafter she never did anything else.

In November of 1951 Nuala presented me with our second son, Rupert. Curiously, he was to become more expert in their field than most of my then colleagues in the intelligence branch, choosing to become a military historian specialising in espionage. He would write some two dozen books under his pen name of Nigel West and several in his own. He was to serve as Conservative MP for Torbay for ten years from 1987.

Although my work was interesting, it no longer commanded the importance of my responsibilities on the Joint Planning Staff. For some time I had been considering how I might stand for the Commons. During the Second World War members of the services could indulge in politics and stand for Parliament, and this happy arrangement continued until 1951.

In 1948 there had been a by-election in Southwark Central, a safe Labour seat in south east London, where the Labour candidate was a young and inexperienced man just down from Oxford, Roy Jenkins. Conservative Central Office gave me some awkward questions to ask, so I went down there with a brother officer, Tony Johnstone, who had been educated at Eton and Sandhurst. We both put questions that flummoxed the candidate and his supporting speaker, Bessie Braddock, who snarled, 'Down here, we don't want clever toffs who have enjoyed an expensive education at Oxford University.' There was a deathly hush, as the only person present fitting that description was Roy.

I had in 1947 been accepted onto the Central Office list of candidates, and in 1950 I had been in the last three for selection for the Northampton constituency. Brigadier Terry Clarke, however, spoilt the entire arrangement by lodging an official complaint of political

Investiture as OBE at Buckingham Palace June 1954. Julian (centre) brought Her Majesty a toy bottle of milk.

General Sir Michael West commanding British forces in the Korean conflict. "It was damn cold."

The Old War Office building – my room was third window right from the centre on the first floor

Photo by Julian Allason

victimisation when he was posted away from Portsmouth, where he was candidate for one of the Parliamentary seats. A major row ensued and it was decided to forbid servicemen from engaging in politics forthwith, I thus found myself having to issue the Army Council Instruction explaining this in time for the General Election of 1951. Although it had been my duty, I took considerable pleasure in disobeying this directive by speaking on a Conservative platform during the election campaign.

Several bright young national servicemen spotted this as a splendid opportunity to get out of the army. They would fight a Parliamentary by-election, and have to be discharged. But I arranged to call them up again as soon as they had lost the by-election, to start all over again as recruits. Enthusiasm for the scheme waned.

My branch of the War Office kept in close touch with the Special Investigations Branch (SIB) of the Military Police, and on one occasion there was a fire at Aldershot where sabotage was suspected. The SIB mounted surveillance, reporting that there were several suspicious characters hanging about dressed in mackintoshes. I was amused to be informed of almost identical reports submitted by the teams from MI5 and Special Branch.

On another occasion I instructed the SIB to visit the Ordnance Depot at Bicester to investigate certain losses. Upon his arrival the SIB man reported at the commanding officer's office, only to witness the CO turn white as a sheet and dictate a confession on a totally different matter. After that, the SIB officer explained why he had really come.

After a record nine years' continuous service in England an overseas posting in 1954 was inevitable. It seemed the moment to retire from the army.

9

London Life

After the birth of our son Julian in May 1948, our small house in Chapel Street became crowded. It was certainly not big enough for Julian's first nanny, the formidable Nurse Watson, who proved much too bossy for us. She soon found a more suitable post with Selwyn Lloyd, whose wife had left him with a daughter to look after. As Foreign Secretary he was living in his official residence at 1 Carlton House Terrace. Selwyn later told me that before the 1959 polls he had informed Nurse Watson that if the Conservatives lost the General Election they would have to leave the next day. She declared that this was quite impossible, so the election must be won.

After one or two failures, Nanny Chable, an army widow, came to us and gave many years of devoted service, and was much loved in return. Our next-door neighbour in London was John Wyndham, the owner of the magnificent Petworth House in Sussex. His son, Max, was the same age as Julian, so Nanny was invited with Julian to Petworth for the weekend. When she returned she reported, 'Madam, it's bigger than Buckingham Palace.'

When our second son, Rupert, arrived in November 1951 we needed a nursemaid and the house proved too small to accommodate us all. Accordingly, we started looking for a larger home, and at last in 1953 we found 15 Cheyne Walk, where the family was to remain for the next fifty years.

After retirement from the army I took over from my father as trustee of several small family trusts, managing property in west London, houses, shops, offices and even a small factory. I had helped my father over this since 1945. The experience gained was of value in the Commons, especially when dealing with the professional bluff of surveyors and estate agents.

An eventful year for us was 1953, as Nuala and I took a furnished cottage at Bembridge, in the Isle of Wight, for two weeks, and liked the village so much that we stayed for two months. I realised it would be cheaper to buy a house rather than rent on this scale, and heard that an attractive but damp Georgian property, Pump Lane House, was on the market. It was under offer to a local resident, Earl St Aldwyn, who already had a house in Bembridge, but whose nanny had objected to sharing the single bathroom. Pump Lane House had two, but luckily for us Nanny St Aldwyn gave in her notice, so Pump Lane House became available and we moved in at Easter 1954.

Bembridge proved ideal for the children, who grew up with the same friends from sandcastles on the beach to dinghy sailing in the harbour. The village was also to acquire a political significance during the Macmillan era, with numerous MPs and ministers maintaining summer homes there. Apart from the St Aldwyns, neighbours and regular visitors included Duncan Sandys, Reggie Bennett, Lord Mancroft, Viscount Hudson, Humphrey Atkins and Peter Rawlinson. Indeed, some wag had claimed that the Prime Minister would have found it easier to call an August Cabinet meeting in Bembridge than in London.

Near the foot of the steps to the front door of Pump Lane House was a small and very muddy pond. Evening visitors turning to wave goodbye were liable to fall in. It became known as the Peers' Pond since so many members of the Upper House became its victims. When Ted Heath visited, we ensured his safety.

Pump Lane House had plenty of room for the family, and two spare double bedrooms, so we had many guests. One year the Spanish Ambassador mentioned that Don Juan, the Pretender to the Spanish throne, was bringing his yacht for Cowes week: could we put up two couples of his entourage? They turned out to be the Duke and Duchess of Medinacelli, his brother and sister-in-law. The Duchess, one of the richest women in Spain, had never undressed in front of her husband, so the girls took one room and the brothers the other. Don Juan's family stayed on his yacht, but when he sailed on the Fastnet race on the Saturday we managed to squeeze in his daughter, the Infanta Pilar, for the night.

Years later, Nuala had our old friend Ayesha, Maharani of Jaipur to stay and they were invited to dine on a magnificent yacht moored off Cowes. As they arrived at the dock Prince Philip emerged from the Royal Yacht Squadron and, upon seeing the Maharani, offered her a lift on his launch. Nuala, thinking he was the boatman asked, 'Have you room for all of us, my man?'. The Prince obliged.

After buying the Bembridge house, our holidays settled into a routine. Early January in Switzerland, usually to St Moritz where the Army Ski Association ran economical package tours; Easter and summer holidays at Bembridge, and at Whitsun somewhere on the Mediterranean. These trips, at a time of severe currency restrictions, were not always easy to finance, and I remember being told that the bar at the Palace Hotel at St Moritz was full of rich Greeks anxious to show their gratitude to Britain by standing drinks to the impoverished English. Naturally I went along to test this proposition and found a friend, June Churchill, former wife of Randolph, sitting with a toadlike Greek. I joined them and waited in vain for the promised drinks to be ordered and finally, in desperation, ordered them myself. When it was clear that there was not going to be a return round, I left, later discovering that the Greek's name was Aristotle Onassis.

St Moritz proved a great success and we were later to make annual visits, staying at Andreas Badrutt's Palace Hotel. This was the social centre of the town, visited in the evenings by everyone, even those with their own chalets. One evening I was dancing with Princess Bismarck, who remarked how vulgar it was to wear imitation diamond earrings, pointing to an Italian woman across the floor. I asked how she knew they were artificial, and she explained that they were bigger than her own gigantic engagement ring. The Italian proved to be the wife of Gianni Agnelli, the owner of Fiat.

On another occasion a drunken Englishman was smoking a cigar while dancing in the Palace bar and the shipping tycoon Stavros Niarchos asked him to put it out. The Englishman refused and the waiters were called to remove him. The other British present, although acknowledging that their compatriot had behaved badly, felt he was being handled too roughly by the waiters and a fight ensued. The next morning Badrutt summoned Colonel Murphy, the Ski Club of Great Britain representative, to inspect the damage. Appalled, Colonel Murphy promised that he would ban all British visitors from the Palace. It was Badrutt's turn to be dismayed, and he besought Murphy to forget the entire incident.

In January 1958 we decided to visit a new ski resort, Alpe d'Huez, with the Bearsteds – Dick, Heather and their two daughters, Felicity and Camilla. Dick was no longer chairman of Shell with a private aircraft at his disposal so we travelled by train. Knowing the difficulty in finding porters, I registered our suitcases through to Grenoble. Upon arrival I was informed that the luggage would not arrive until the next day, and would then have to be cleared by French customs. Unfortunately, I was also informed, the only customs officer was away sick. Grenoble's Shell representative was on the platform to greet him. I soon discovered the chief qualification of an oil company representative – the ability to fix anything – when I was invited to hand him the keys to the luggage. The next morning he drove it up to Alpe d'Huez with the compliments of Shell.

One Whitsun weekend we came down for dinner at Eden Roc, on Cap d'Antibes, when we found the suave man-about-town Charles Oppenheim in the bar with a young French girl. After drinks we went in to supper, and Nuala said, 'That French girl was dining with us last week.' 'Nonsense,' I replied. 'All those French girls look alike.' Meanwhile, the girl was protesting to Charles, 'You promised me that we would know no one if I came here. I was dining with those people last week.' She promptly took the next train back to Paris.

From the age of six, Julian and Arabella, the daughter of Randolph and June Churchill, were great friends, so Julian was invited to stay at Stour near East Bergholt in Suffolk. I sent him off with £5 to tip the butler, which Randolph promptly borrowed. But he returned it to Julian at the end of the visit, with 100% interest, so Julian thought moneylending a useful trade. Staying with Randolph at his chalet in Switzerland four years later, Julian had to share with Arabella the task of reading to her father what he had written that day of his life of Winston. Julian was entrusted with the manuscript and instructions to deliver it to the publisher in London – and another tenner. A career as a courier seemed to beckon.

The Jaipurs had by now acquired a house in Berkshire as a base for the English season. One spring Jai told me he was forming a polo team with the Dominican playboy Porfirio Rubirosa, and that the third player also had a high handicap, so they needed a low-handicap player as the fourth. I promptly accepted, but Jai then asked if I had the ponies. Surely, I replied, Rubirosa would sponsor us, but was told, 'Unfortunately Rubirosa is between wives.'

Rubirosa's first marriage had been to the daughter of Trujillo, the Dominican dictator, who appointed him a diplomat. Infidelity caused his banishment, during which Rubirosa sold passports to Jews fleeing Europe. Marrying the tobacco heiress, Doris Duke, in 1947 he had been given a French chateau, a private aircraft, five Ferraris and half a million dollars in cash. Wedding Barbara Hutton six years later, he did even better. That marriage lasted 53 days.

When asked if he ever worked, Rubirosa explained that he did not have time to do so. This was not entirely surprising, as he contrived to fit in affairs with many of Hollywood's leading ladies, including Dolores del Rio, Ava Gardner, Zsa Zsa Gabor, Veronica Lake and Kim Novak, not to mention Eva Peron. While not conventionally handsome, Porfirio was undoubtedly very fit and possessed abundant energy and Latin charm. He shared my love of motor sport and had raced in Formula One and completed the Le Mans twenty-four-hour race. Off the race track his favourite car was a gull-wing Mercedes. It was, however, Rubirosa's reputation as the last of the great Latin lovers that sealed his fame, although the newspapers of the time never referred to his physical attributes.

My sights were now firmly set upon the House of Commons where several friends already had seats. In those days the worlds of politics, the arts and what survived of high society intertwined. We went to many parties but two proved memorable. Jai and Ayesha threw a huge party in London for their twenty-fifth wedding anniversary and the night before gave a dinner dance at their house at Windlesham, Berkshire, for eighteen close friends. We drove down with Lord George Scott and his wife Molly Bishop, the artist. Among the guests were the Queen and Prince Philip. I did not ask her to dance, but perhaps I should have. George did, but then he was the brother of her Aunt Alice, the Duchess of Gloucester.

We were invited by Jack and Drue Heinz to an evening river party in London. We embarked at Westminster Pier, and steamed upstream as far as Richmond. Here Drue explained that on the eastern leg to Greenwich we would be served a Cockney supper of cockles, mussels and whelks. Faces fell. On our way downstream we called at Westminster Pier to pick up latecomers, but most guests streamed ashore. Drue explained that the party was not over yet, to mumbled replies of, 'Terribly sorry, another engagement', and there were few left to enjoy the whelks.

In 1954 I was short-listed for the constituency of the Wrekin. The flamboyant Bill Yates was chosen instead of the quieter John Peel or me. It was made clear that the presence of a wife was essential, but Yates and his wife were parting. She stayed with him until he was elected and then left, to the annoyance of the selection committee. He managed, however, to hold the seat for eleven years. In the chamber, Yates was an intermittent nuisance with his ill-judged interruptions. When President Kennedy died, tributes were paid by the Prime Minister, the Leader of the Opposition, Sir Winston Churchill, and, as an anti-climax, Yates. It was the last time Winston spoke in the chamber, and, happily, he was lucid and relevant. It was a moment to savour before one squirmed.

In 1955 I managed to find a constituency to fight the General Election of that year; it was a hopeless seat, Hackney Central. Much of Hackney consisted of terraced houses of three floors and a basement with a separate family living on each floor. Frequently in the basement there would be an elderly English couple with a picture of Winston Churchill on the wall. They were there because they liked to have their own front door, and although they admired Winston, this did not mean they voted Conservative.

A Jewish tenant of mine ran a restaurant in Oxford Street, but always seemed to have difficulty paying his rent. Perhaps I was too lenient with him, but he expressed his gratitude by coming to canvass for me, and this prompted considerable excitement at the news that the Tories were canvassing in Yiddish. Many friends came to canvass after work in the City: they were met by an undressing squad, who confiscated bowler hats and umbrellas, and wound a muffler on to conceal the stiff white collars.

As was the tradition during the campaign, a local vicar arranged and chaired a public meeting for the three candidates, Tory, Labour and Communist, giving each an opportunity to address the audience and answer questions from the floor. During a lull in the questions he intervened to ask what was the relevance of the Beatitudes to politics. I replied, 'Blessed are the peacemakers. Anthony Eden is in Malaysia now seeking a peace treaty in the Far East.' This seemed a reasonable response, but the Communist candidate on the platform whispered in my ear, 'What are the B attitudes he was asking about?'

Of course, Hackney was unwinnable for the Tories and the objective was simply to gain some experience in campaigning and achieve a creditable result that would help me to gain a more attractive constituency. The sitting MP, predictably, was returned but with his majority reduced, while I surprised myself by polling more than 15,000 votes. I began the search for a new seat, having learnt that even in the most improbable places, such as east London, there were then plenty of Conservative supporters to be encouraged.

In order to gain political experience, I joined Kensington Council. I was equally qualified for Chelsea or Westminster, but Kensington had a powerful Labour opposition. Several of my friends were on Westminster Council, including Raine, then Lady Lewisham, and Patrick de Laszlo. His father, the noted Hungarian portrait painter, when he was given British nationality, kissed his lawyer, Charles Russell, on both cheeks. Russell responded, 'Sir, remember that you are now an Englishman.' Raine deserves everyone's gratitude for preserving Inigo Jones's Piazza at Covent Garden, which would otherwise have been redeveloped into tower blocks when the vegetable market left.

A fellow councillor at Kensington was Ian Perceval, later Solicitor General. When we were both elected to the Commons in 1959, he immediately resigned from the council. I remained for a total of nine years, appreciating being at the cutting edge of London politics.

Before Hemel Hempstead came over my horizon, I had been selected to fight the London County Council election of 1958, for what was thought to be the safe seat of Dulwich. But when the election came, Duncan Sandys, then housing minister, had just brought into law his Rent Act, increasing the rents of private tenants. Unsurprisingly, there were rather more private tenants than landlords in Dulwich, and I was rejected. But for the Rent Act, I should have had the prospect of being a member of three tiers of government at the same time.

Dulwich returned three members, so we three Tory candidates shared the platform at public meetings, and between us contrived to answer almost any question, even, 'What is government policy on Women's Institutes?' I should have answered, 'benevolent', but there was more to it than that. When asked what was a fair rate of interest, I replied 'Three per cent' (loud cheers), 'plus the rate of inflation' (groans). We were not to know that we had just entered four years of nil inflation under the new Chancellor, Derick Heathcote-Amory. Years later he told me that the cost of living index was exactly the same the day he became Chancellor as the day he left office.

Sir Charles MacAndrew, the MP for North Ayrshire and Bute, and a friend of the family since Ayrshire days, told me in 1957 that he was

Macmillan visits Hemel Hempstead Oct 1959. "I expect to win here,
Prime Minister".

Julian, Nuala, James and Rupert at Cheyne Walk, 1959.

Alec Home visits Hemel, October 1964. "Welcome to my Constituency, Prime Minister".

Edward Heath comes to Hemel, February 1974. "Welcome to the Constituency, Ted".

retiring at the next election, and offered me his seat. I eagerly accepted, and asked when I should come to Scotland. He said there was no hurry, because there the retiring member nominates his successor. However, a month or two later he told me to forget it, as a rather important person had asked him for his constituency, and he could not refuse. The following week the newspapers announced that the Scottish war hero Fitzroy Maclean was to resign as MP for Lancaster in order to seek his fortune north of the border. Thus I escaped many years of weekly journeys to Scotland.

In post-war years quite a few Conservative MPs were due to inherit a peerage, but served on from a sense of duty, and sometimes at their own expense. For instance, George Lambert, the MP for North Cornwall, had to guarantee to pay the expenses of a by-election if his father should die. When this happened in 1957, he asked if I was interested in taking over his seat, but I declined because it would have meant standing as a National Liberal, at this time allied to but not yet united with the Conservative Party.

Some time before this, Viscount Hinchinbroke, known to all simply as 'Hinch', invited me to join a small group of potential candidates who dined monthly at his Westminster house to discuss political developments. Hinch, the son of the Earl of Sandwich, was a tall, elegant figure. He claimed to be a Whig, representing the interests of the country against those of the urban and industrial Tories. He was passionately hostile to the European Common Market. He sat in the Commons on the front bench below the gangway, so that he could snarl at close quarters at the most extreme left-wingers. Of those who attended Hinch's dinners regularly, only Sir Edward Boyle and I were to prove successful as candidates. At one meeting, Hinch asked Woodrow Wyatt, a Labour MP, when he was joining the Conservatives. Wyatt replied, 'If you had found me, you would not be seeking me.' Boyle, from his encyclopaedic brain, recited the correct line from Proverbs (8:17), which rather qualified what had been quoted.

Years later I was in Wyatt's house, drinking champagne from a silver goblet, and asked him how, as a socialist, he could own racehorses? 'But I want everyone to own racehorses,' he replied. I had considered Woodrow a friend, and he often attended our parties at Cheyne Walk, but he was left off the invitation list when his wife, Moorea, wrote a satirical article about one of our parties in a Banbury newspaper.

Evidently she had not reckoned with the efficiency of my press cuttings service.

In 1962 Hinch's father died, so there had to be a by-election in South Dorset, and as well as the Conservative an anti-Common Market candidate also stood. Hinch did not take a tactful holiday abroad, but true to his principles, supported the anti-European candidate. The Tory vote was split, and Labour won. Soon afterwards, Anthony Wedgwood Benn, having inherited the unwanted title of Viscount Stansgate, achieved a change in the law allowing a peer to disclaim his title in order to stand for the Commons.

I begged Hinch to remain in the Lords so that his wise counsel might continue, but his love was of the Commons, in which he was convinced that he could find a seat and return; thus he disclaimed his title. Central Office, however, considered him a traitor and he was never again selected.

I always enjoyed a shooting weekend, so when Hinch invited me to Maperton, his lovely house in Dorset, I gladly accepted. The shooting proved not quite on a par with that at Blenheim, for instead of beaters to drive the birds towards us there were several tenant farmers armed with shotguns. The only pheasant we saw all day was shot at close range as it started to fly towards the line of guns by the beating farmer who had put it up.

Finally, in 1958, I heard that Lady Davidson, the wife of the legendary member of Stanley Baldwin's Cabinet, and later Party Chairman, Viscount Davidson, was to retire from the relatively safe seat of Hemel Hempstead. The constituency was made up of a new town in Hertfordshire coupled with a large rural and urban area, and was conveniently close to London.

I was invited to lunch with old Lord Davidson, which turned out to be the selection procedure, and during the course of it he asked my opinion of the Commonwealth. Suitably briefed, I replied that, 'I prefer to call it the Empire,' whereupon he turned to me and assured me, 'The seat's yours.' Thus I was installed as the prospective Parliamentary candidate for a very winnable constituency.

In the summer of 1959, however, Crossbencher, the political columnist on the *Sunday Express*, ran an amusing series on the most bogus election candidates. For the Liberals he chose Jeremy Thorpe, Robert Maxwell for Labour, and myself for the Tories, flatteringly describing me as, 'a Chelsea playboy dressed in immaculate tweeds.'

A somewhat foppish Etonian, Jeremy Thorpe was given to rather dandified attire and other colourful eccentricities. He was also a fine mimic, and like some other politicians, adapted his accent to suit his company. His broad West Country accent went down well in North Devon and he rose to be leader of the Liberal Party, with an offer of a place in Ted Heath's Cabinet in February 1974. Before long he crashed into oblivion, having been acquitted of the attempted murder of his male lover, Norman Scott, who had been blackmailing him. The plot to silence Scott was held to have extended to much of the Liberal leadership, and had even been financed, albeit unwittingly, by a wealthy supporter who had sent large sums to Thorpe direct, by-passing the party's treasurer. Although he was cleared of the criminal charges, Thorpe was ruined and retired from public life.

Robert Maxwell also had secrets to conceal. He had been born in Ruthenia, later part of post-war Czechoslovakia, but had been commissioned into the British Army during the war. Posted to Berlin, and while still serving, he had become involved in the black market and had acquired a publishing business, Pergamon, which would make him a fortune but leave numerous investors penniless. The attraction of Pergamon was an extensive back-list of academic and scientific articles which had been banned from publication during the Nazi era. Maxwell published them in journals that were subscribed to by most of the world's university libraries, and gained a substantial income for very little effort. In later years Pergamon would exploit the need of many academics to get their papers published, even if they were not remunerated. The result was a guaranteed income, paid for in a subscription on 1 January, with no shortage of material to print at negligible editorial cost.

When Maxwell had made his first fortune he announced that he was going into Parliament. 'Don't be silly', a friend had said, 'The Tories will never have you.' 'I know,' replied Maxwell, 'that's why I'm joining Labour.' Sure enough, he was adopted for Buckingham, a constituency consisting of the town and many rural villages around it. During the 1959 election campaign, the villages were visited by three identical Land Rovers, each carrying a portly figure wearing his trademark duffle coat, and decorated with a placard proclaiming, 'Hear Maxwell speak.' Loudspeakers blasted out Maxwell's voice, recorded on tape. Thus he conveyed the impression of being in three places at the same time, a feat entirely unmatched by his opponents, who marvelled at his energy and at the attention Labour was paying to the outlying villages, hitherto considered unimportant. Unsuspecting of this combination of substitution, impersonation and the application of modern technology (and a blind disregard for the meagre election expenses allowed by the law), Maxwell's handsome win went unchallenged by the authorities.

Later, when the champagne socialist became unpopular with the local Labour party, there was a motion to de-select him. Mysteriously, every village formed a Labour branch and demanded the right to send a delegate to the General Management Committee, all of whom somehow voted for Maxwell, thereby ensuring he was retained as the candidate.

Once in the Commons, Maxwell used every ploy to get his name known. His surname, of course, appeared just after Harold Macmillan's in the Hansard index, and in order to gain more entries he adopted the practice of interrupting members for the sole purpose of showing that he had participated in a particular debate. Whereas others, by convention, had to wait in the chamber to be called by the Speaker, and attend the entire debate, Maxwell would sail in, wait a couple of minutes until an opportunity arose, and then make his intervention. This behaviour was considered poor manners, but he was so thick-skinned and so persistent that the kind of Members' Tea Room criticism that would have chastened anyone else carried little sanction.

In the 1964 Parliament, while I was making the wind-up speech from the Opposition front bench in a debate on housing, Maxwell sauntered in and, characteristically, soon interrupted me with his intervention. I managed to make a fool of him, and both sides of the House laughed. Apparently missing the joke, he joined in the laughter too. Clearly he regarded the Commons as a mere means to furthering his own interests, without regard for anyone else. He brushed off the most scathing reports about his business dealings, and when eventually he became proprietor of the *Daily Mirror*, he looted the newspaper's pension fund.

Maxwell was to die in mysterious circumstances in the Atlantic, apparently the victim of an accident on his yacht, engendering a titanic financial scandal that would engulf several City institutions. His insurers, chaired by Robin Warrender, held a financial post-mortem attended by his biographer, Tom Bower, and both my sons. The tentative, if improbable conclusion reached was that a massive attack of flatulence had propelled Maxwell over the guardrail of his yacht and into the sea. He also left the Commons devoid of an excellent wine cellar. Having been appointed Chairman of the Commons Catering Committee on the pledge that he would end the many years of embarrassing losses suffered by the Refreshments Department, he had sold off the cellar stock to balance the books, much of it to himself.

Maxwell stood out in the Commons because he was there so obviously to further his own gargantuan ambitions. In those days the pay was minuscule, the hours long, the facilities primitive and the tax-free allowances non-existent. Backbenchers did not have their own rooms, and shared the use of a few telephones in the corridors. Waistcoats and striped trousers were the uniform so beloved by Giles the cartoonist, and a media interview was a relatively rare event, unless it was published in the local newspaper following the opening of the Little Gaddesden annual fete. Constituency mail received personal replies, and MPs followed other professions, few of them connected with their Parliamentary duties, often bringing to bear useful real world experience.

Lord and Lady Melchett, Julian and Sonia, had been friends for some years. They came down to Bembridge and we stayed with them in Norfolk and Majorca. Julian's grandfather had been the first chairman of ICI, and he was now the vigorous chairman of the British Steel Corporation. Blessed with restless energy and an ability to think on his feet Julian had enjoyed considerable success in defending his industry from political interference. Sonia supported this endeavour by hosting parties at which the guestlist was so glittering that Cabinet ministers often felt themselves the least important persons there.

On their first visit to New York, Nuala gave the Melchetts an introduction to her cousin, Emmett Blot, a millionaire resident there, and he invited them to dinner. It was the last day of their stay before embarking the next morning on the *Queen Mary*. After dinner baccarat was played, but they had little money left and Sonia soon lost her share. But Julian started to win, and at the expense of the Duchess of Windsor, who was unamused. So Julian tried to lose, and consequently won all the more. The result was that Sonia had several thousand dollars to spend on Fifth Avenue and only two hours in which to do so. There was no time for clothes, and she had to settle for a necklace from Tiffany's.

When the General Election of 1959 opened, there were public meetings in every town and village to be addressed, almost always well attended. Julian Melchett offered to come and speak for me, on the subject of agriculture, so I told my agent to arrange it for a suitable meeting. But when we arrived at a village near Tring, there were only two in the audience and the meeting had to be abandoned. We went on to a full meeting at Tring, where the Melchetts had to sit in the audience. I gave my constituency agent hell.

Polling day was very tiring, as I visited every committee room and polling station in a very widespread constituency. Our chairman invited us to watch the early results at his home in Harpenden, but we pleaded exhaustion. We then drove to London to the *Daily Telegraph* party at the Savoy. The next morning, when we arrived to attend the count, my chairman enquired if we had gone straight to bed. I said we had just called in at one party. I did not know that on the front page of the *Telegraph* was a photograph of the party, with me in the foreground.

10

Parliament

The 1959 General Election resulted in a large number of new Tory members, so promotion was slow, with only Margaret Thatcher and Basil de Ferranti being appointed junior ministers in the five years before the next election. Life on the government back-benches could be quite dull, as the whips discouraged speeches in order to get on with the business.

I was puzzled that Cheshire sent us such charming MPs as John Foster, Peter Roberts and Jack Temple. Whereas Kent suffered buffoons such as Freddy Burden and Billy Rees-Davies. But there were exceptions. Bill Deedes definitely fell into the Cheshire category. He would later employ my son Julian as technology columnist at the *Daily Telegraph*, although Julian wondered how often the great editor ever progressed beyond his first paragraph.

Early in the first session, Margaret Thatcher was lucky enough to win a place in the ballot, which entitled her to present a private member's bill. I had heard that she was impressive, so I went to a meeting at which she described her bill with great clarity. Someone asked an awkward question, and the reply was 'That is dealt with in clause 9, sub-section 3, which reads as follows —' I was not the only one to be lost in admiration. It was said that when she was an undergraduate at Oxford working for a chemistry degree, she decided that she wished to enter Parliament but was totally unqualified. She worked out that to succeed she must become a barrister, marry a successful businessman, give him two children to keep him happy, and then would be a suitable candidate. Such was her efficiency that she presented him with twins to save time.

Another exponent of efficiency was Ernest Marples, who maintained a house in Eccleston Street, Belgravia. This was a main traffic route, so he fitted treble glazing to the windows. The house had three kitchens, because he and Ruth, his wife, liked to cook simultaneously. The third was for the staff. Appointed Minister of Transport, on his first day he asked the Permanent Under-Secretary what was the worst problem confronting the ministry. The answer was London traffic. Asking for an example, he was told that the preceding Christmas it had taken a bus thirty minutes to travel from Marble Arch to Oxford Circus and that it would take forty minutes next Christmas. Marples said he had heard enough. The following day he produced his plan for double yellow lines to indicate 'no parking'. A pre-war Minister of Transport, Hore-Belisha, was still remembered for Belisha beacons, but Ernest disclaimed 'Marples lines', perhaps due to sensitivity that his old firm, Marples Ridgeway, was building some of the new motorways, and favouritism was sometimes suggested.

When Labour took power in 1964, Marples would spend a year in America studying technology. He returned and wrote a paper for Conservative Central Office, the importance of which eluded them, even though Harold Wilson had just won by promising to galvanise Britain with the 'white heat of the technological revolution'. When Marples told me this, I exclaimed in surprise, 'But you must be one of the best informed on technology in Britain?'. To which he modestly replied, 'I *am* the best informed.'

In October 1960 I was the first of the new intake to be appointed a Parliamentary Private Secretary (PPS). In those days the role of the PPS was more akin to a junior minister, and only the most senior ministers were allowed to enjoy the unpaid help of a PPS. Departments were also much smaller, and the ministerial teams usually consisted only of the Cabinet minister, of whom there were probably only twenty, his deputy being a single minister of state, and then a junior minister. There is no comparison to the legions of Parliamentary under-secretaries of state in today's huge administrations where a large proportion of the Parliamentary party is on the government payroll.

To my delight, I was appointed PPS to Jack Profumo, who had been chosen by Harold Macmillan to be his Secretary of State for War, in charge of the army in the War Office. This was in July 1960, a time when the three major services had their own departments, with a First Lord of the Admiralty and an Air Minister as well. Harold Watkinson sat in the Cabinet as Minister of Defence, a position created by Winston

Churchill when he had taken on the dual role of Prime Minister and Minister of Defence in the dark days of May 1940. Thus Jack, who had been elected to the Commons first during the war in a by-election at Kettering in 1940, and then in 1950 for Stratford-on-Avon, needed someone who understood the ways of the War Office. Although Secretary of State for War, and of equal rank to the Minister for Air and the First Lord of the Admiralty, Jack had not served in the Cabinet. His previous ministerial experience had been in Transport, the Colonial Office and the Foreign Office, where he had been promoted Minister of State after just three months as Parliamentary Under-Secretary of State. Aged only forty-five, Jack was undoubtedly seen as a high-flyer.

My first task each morning at the War Office, where I had a room next to Jack's, was to go through his in-tray and tell him what letters drafted by the civil servants *not* to sign. This was, at first, unpopular with his private secretary, but the civil service soon came to see that it was better not to send devious replies to letters of inquiry, and during the three years we were to work together we achieved an unprecedented level of co-operation between the civil servants, the military and the politicians. One day the Adjutant-General told me that his department was nearly overwhelmed by inquiries from MPs, so could I please arrange a reduction? I explained that an inquisitive Parliament was essential to provide a watchdog on the activities of all governments whether benign – as ours was – or extremist.

Britain was in a period of disengagement, with Prime Minister Harold Macmillan committed to ending colonialism, but we still had worldwide responsibilities and garrisons across the globe. The trick was to settle local disputes and honour our promises of self-determination at a speed that would allow new administrations to be installed without the destabilising consequences of over-hasty withdrawal. There were British troops in the Far East, the Middle East, the Mediterranean, Africa and the Caribbean, and our task was to sustain them and offer security to the emerging independent states while still maintaining the ability to deploy our forces in a counter-insurgency role should the need arise.

Despite Britain still having national service it was clear that an entirely professional and re-equipped army was needed to meet the threat of Soviet tanks rolling across the plains of northern Germany, or react to the intervention of Marxist guerrillas in Commonwealth countries. The War Office was one of the most important departments of state, and Jack was a dynamic, ambitious minister who was a pleasure to work with. He was also attractive and slightly flirtatious, and married to the beautiful actress Valerie Hobson. A rich man, having inherited an insurance business, and the holder of an Italian title, Baron Profumo, he was at the centre of power and of London's glittering social life.

My re-enlistment scheme of 1951 for dealing with national servicemen who went to fight by-elections had worked well for ten years, until – horror of horrors – a young Welshman named Michael Heseltine won his by-election and was elected to the Commons. This practice had been described by Winston Churchill as 'using the House of Commons as a public convenience'. Clearly a new policy was required, but could not be found until I suggested that the obligation of military service should overrule the civil right to stand for Parliament. The agreement of the Opposition was essential, and as this was to be a matter of electoral procedure, and therefore a Home Office issue, the Shadow Home Secretary, Patrick Gordon-Walker, was consulted. He gave his approval, but he evidently forgot to tell George Brown, Labour's thirsty Shadow Defence Minister. When the Home Secretary announced the new policy in the House, the tipsy George Brown leapt up and promised to fight this disgraceful policy tooth and nail. He was pulled down by his coat-tails, and Gordon-Walker accepted the change on behalf of the Opposition.

As a skilled politician, Jack understood the need for public relations. He ordered that rather than being a dead-end sinecure the job of head of PR at the War Office should be given to a serving major-general with good career prospects, and Lord Monckton was duly chosen. He and I studied the press each day, alert for trouble. Our fathers had been friends in the First World War and Gilbert Monckton was a natural communicator with the gift of plain speaking. As we all knew, good news is dull, but bad news sells newspapers. It would not be long before we began to regard the press as a potentially dangerous adversary, and the roots of what was to become a bitter conflict are to be found in some of the events that preoccupied us at the War Office during those early days.

All the newspapers employed representatives in Germany, where the occasional court-martial offered potentially colourful copy. The army had long adopted the practice of displaying advance notices of all forthcoming courts-martial, and the reporters covering the British Army of the Rhine (BAOR) invariably deputed one man to scan the notice board for the rest of his colleagues. On one occasion, however, he was away on assignment when a juicy court-martial was announced, so the entire press corps missed it. Protesting that the usual notice had not been given, they implied that the army had attempted to conceal it. A major rumpus followed as the War Office issued a denial, and a Parliamentary Question on the subject was tabled in the House. The Opposition was a little slow to understand precisely what had happened so Jack explained that 'the press had missed a trick.' The Fleet Street editors were infuriated by this apparently justified attack on the competence of their profession, and the reporters responsible were rebuked.

The press always has the last word, and so the journalists nursed their revenge. The opportunity arose when a Scottish battalion stationed in Minden went out on the town and their celebrations got a little out of hand. The local mayor had denounced them as, 'poison dwarfs', and the story was carried with enthusiasm by the newspapers. In the midst of this media field-day Jack called a conference of the Chief of the General Staff, the Adjutant-General and the Commander-in-Chief Germany.

As Secretary of State, Jack chaired the meeting, and when the generals had left I asked what had been decided. Jack told me a nine o'clock curfew was to be imposed on the BAOR. I objected that this would be regarded as unacceptable by the troops, who would see this as a collective punishment. I suggested that if the curfew was moved to ten o'clock, it could be presented as an attempt to improve efficiency, and Jack took the point, recalled the generals, and settled it.

On another awkward occasion the War Office nearly became the victim of a pretty actress in search of publicity. She persuaded a tabloid gossip columnist to introduce her to Jack at a drinks party, suggesting she could improve the dowdy image of the Women's Royal Army Corps. Uninterested, Jack had turned away, but the next day the paper reported that he had agreed to her proposal, thereby suggesting that the Secretary of State implicitly acknowledged that the WRAC had a poor image that needed to be improved with some glamour. Such a suggestion was bound to cause great offence, and the result was another Parliamentary Question, which concluded with the observation from Reggie Paget, the Shadow Army Minister, delivered with a terrible leer, 'All that seems to have happened was that the Minister met a very pretty girl.' The crisis passed, but the incident had helped gain Jack a reputation as a ladies' man, or at least someone with an eye for a pretty girl.

My busy Parliamentary schedule included accompanying the Secretary of State on most of his visits to military establishments, where he invariably created a memorable impression. On my own visit to the Hemel Hempstead telephone exchange I discussed the problems faced by the local postmaster, within whose remit it fell. Beside us sat a row of girls connecting calls manually by plugging cables into sockets. As I watched their impressive performance I knew that if Jack had been present he would have replaced one of the operators and caused chaos by connecting the wrong callers – but his visit would never have been forgotten. The only occasion I ever saw him at a loss was when we inspected the Army Pay Office. The huge building was filled with giant computers with flashing lights and whirling reels of tape: there was simply no opportunity for Jack to interfere.

In January 1962 we went on a tour of the Persian Gulf and after visiting Muscat and Aden we flew down to inspect Kenya and Zanzibar, all then under British influence or control, and none the worse for that. The Persian Gulf was then friendly, with the exception of Iraq. At the western end oil-rich Kuwait and Bahrain had been members of the Commonwealth, and there were still strong British forces in Bahrain, and a defensive treaty with Kuwait. We stayed at Bahrain, where Jack could check on our ability to support Kuwait at short notice. Then we moved to the eastern end of the Gulf, where no oil had yet been found.

There the five emirates with allegiance to the Commonwealth had come to an agreement that if one struck oil, the profits should be divided into six, the extra share going to the oil producer. In the meantime, the ruler had at least the inestimable privilege of nominating applicants for British passports.

We stayed at Dubai, the smallest but most populated of the five states. It had a port conducting a prosperous trade by dhow with Karachi, including smuggled gold. We had lunch with the ruler, Sheikh Rashid, in a tent in the desert at which baby camel was served. It was probably more comfortable there than in his palace in the port. The high commissioner had briefed us on the need to burp in appreciation of this feast, but one of our number was too well brought up to be able to comply. A ventriloquist was added to the party.

Enoch Powell, the polymath demonstrates the pogo stick to his family.

Jack Profumo in Muscat on our tour of the Gulf in January 1962. Jack proved a hit with sheikhs and British troops alike.

Norman Tebbit with Margaret Thatcher. "At least I can trust the Hemel Hempstead
Mafia, Norman."

Audience with the Lion
of Judah 1971. Emperor
Haile Selassie thawed
upon being reminded of
his exile in Bath.

A year or so later, oil was found in Qatar, Dubai carefully investing its share in commercial development to become a trading state of world importance. Sheikh Rashid's sons, heirs to impoverishment, became famous racehorse owners in England, the Maktoum brothers.

In Muscat, the 22nd Special Air Service had just carried out a successful operation against communist rebels, although the deployment of the regiment had not been publicised in England. The SAS was a small, self-contained unit ideally suited to working against bands of irregulars and guerrillas, and its effectiveness had been demonstrated in Malaya, where the regular squadrons had been re-formed after they had been disbanded following the Second World War. Their reputation had proved fully justified here too, for they had adopted the tactics of the enemy, living off the land and infiltrating the local terrain, however inhospitable, in small teams accompanied by a doctor, preparing ambushes and winning the loyalty of the local inhabitants. The Radfan mountains were rather different to the jungles of south-east Asia, but the SAS had adapted to the environment and isolated the Yemeni-backed rebels.

We heard that Muscat's Sultan had two pairs of eyelids, and if he opened both you died. When we had lunch with him, there were two guards on the door with drawn scimitars, so I was careful not to point my toe at him, a sign of disrespect in Arabia. He had, I noted, very droopy eyelids, so perhaps if he opened them fully in anger the guards would take the hint. I suggested that his beautiful coastline could be a tourist paradise, as it now is, but he said that if there were to be any development in his country someone would want to take it from him. Two years later this came true when vast oil deposits were found, his state became hugely wealthy, and he was deposed in a coup d'etat.

On our way to Kenya, through Aden, we stayed with the Governor, Sir Charles Johnstone, translator of Pushkin and, at the other end of the intellectual scale, a member of the Imperial Poona Yacht Club, that eccentric organisation whose members must never have been to Poona. Johnstone entertained himself by shooting at flower bowls on the parapets of Government House, a pastime that irritated the sentries on duty below.

Life at the centre of politics during the Macmillan era was not all scandal and excitement. Macmillan's manner, that of an Edwardian landowner, sat at odds with his pose as the grandson of a crofter. In fact his impenetrable sang-froid masked hidden pain, rooted in his experiences in the Great War and enduring marital difficulties. So, at least it seemed to me. Prime ministers in those days enjoyed a personal respect that largely transcended political boundaries, and Macmillan was both principled and a shrewd political operator. But a man of the people he was not, and that left him vulnerable to the charge of being out of touch. More importantly his limited personal empathy made it difficult for him to understand the subtler motivation of others. This was to have important consequences as events unfolded at which I found myself occupying a ringside seat.

The tradition of Cabinet government had received a fillip during the all-party wartime administration, and under Macmillan this continued to an extent that might surprise observers of present day politics. I recall being told by a minister what had happened in Cabinet that morning. Enoch Powell, then Minister of Health, described in dramatic terms, the dangers of smoking. One by one, around the Cabinet table, ministers stubbed out their cigarettes. All agreed that smoking must be banned, until it came to the Chancellor, Reggie Maudling, who pointed out the cost of pensions for longer-living seniors, and that the loss of revenue from tobacco would mean a huge increase in other taxes. Much relieved, everyone lit up again.

It had been no surprise to bump into Enoch in the Central Lobby, and he had seemed equally unfazed to re-encounter me. For this was still the era of the soldier-politician that had opened after the Great War. For some who had survived it was a means of being of further service – and once again at the centre of events. For others, like Enoch, it represented a natural progression of their upward trajectory. Military experience was valued, not so much for loyalty and party discipline (former officers were, if anything, less likely to follow political orders slavishly) as for administrative expertise and leadership qualities. In addition Enoch bore the mantle of the thinker.

Surprisingly, given his later reputation as the prophet of immigration disaster, Enoch prided himself upon his rapport with Asian constituents and upon his command of Urdu, painstakingly acquired during our time in India. During one campaign he strode up to a small group of Indian women and addressed them fluently for several minutes without interruption. This was not entirely surprising as they were Gujarati speakers and understandably baffled.

In the long summer recess, the Parliamentary pressure was off and I was able to spend much of August with Nuala and the family in Bembridge. In September 1962 I was invited to go on a lecture tour in the United States visiting far-flung cities, quite unaware that the world was about to be plunged into crisis. I was warned that when in America's Middle-West I should explain that I was English, otherwise 'they will think from your accent you are from Boston and punch you on the nose'. Happily no such incident occurred.

In Chicago I was invited on to the 'Kuk Show', a popular television chat programme that ran for three hours on Saturday evenings. Kuk seemed to like my ability to talk at length on almost any subject and I stayed the full three hours as other guests came and went. My host told me that his nightmare guest had been Lord Attlee, who replied, 'Humph' to every question put to him. One of my fellow guests was an Indian Member of Parliament, who said it would be quite wrong for the United States to invade Cuba, which was then preparing to install Soviet nuclear missiles. I reminded him that India had just invaded Goa but, unimpressed by the parallel, he simply responded, 'Oh, but that was quite different.' Perhaps he meant that the Portugese colony had offered no threat to India.

Another guest was Oleg Cassini, Mrs Kennedy's couturier; the conversation turned to men's fashion, and the reason for sleeve buttons on men's jackets. I said they were useful to unbutton and turn back the sleeves while washing one's hands, as I then proceeded to demonstrate, as did Oleg, but most likely he and I were the only two men in Chicago wearing Savile Row suits with buttonable sleeves. Although I much enjoyed my trip to the city, I was shaken to learn that a week after my visit an American admiral, taking the same route back to our hotel after dinner one evening, had been murdered for the few dollars he had on him.

Such trivialities were soon swept aside as intermediate-range ballistic missile sites were detected in Cuba, and President Kennedy went on coast-to-coast television to announce the imposition of a quarantine on all ships bound for Fidel Castro's island. Suddenly the world seemed on the brink of an atomic exchange as the President despatched an envoy to London to brief Harold Macmillan on the photographic evidence obtained by reconnaissance overflights of the missile sites. The Prime Minister, General de Gaulle and Chancellor Adenauer all gave their support to the immediate ban on all further deliveries of offensive weapons to Cuba. The world waited, hastily preparing contingency plans, while Nikita Khrushchev pondered the Kremlin's response.

As soon as my lecture tour was over I had returned to England to be at my post, where I immediately received a disturbing intelligence report that the Americans were poised to start World War III with a limited nuclear attack. The Prime Minister received this briefing from Major-General Sir Kenneth Strong, director of the Joint Intelligence Bureau, on 19 November before the crisis had been resolved. So alarmed was he that he had a copy delivered to the Queen without delay. While I had been engaged on my tour the US Navy, it now emerged, had been conducting a rehearsal in North Carolina for the invasion of Cuba, again without informing us, apparently in anticipation of our objections. The order for the exercise had been given when Castro had shown signs of reneging on the Soviet agreement to remove the missiles and Ilyushin-28 bombers. Evidently the 'maximum leader' had been infuriated by compromise and had voiced his opposition to what the Kremlin had agreed with Washington. The sabre-rattling along the eastern seaboard of the United States had been intended as a none too subtle warning to Havana, and the point was taken.

The American intelligence briefings given to President Kennedy had anticipated a Soviet move against Berlin, and the doctrine recommended a pre-emptive bomber strike against Soviet inter-continental ballistic missile sites. Our own assessments were altogether less confident that all the launch sites had been identified, and far from certain that they could all be rendered harmless in one attack. Macmillan and the Foreign Secretary, Lord Home, were shocked to discover that consultation by our closest ally had proved to be a sham, a realisation that was all the more grave when we knew how close we had come to a nuclear exchange, the outcome of which was, in our estimation, far from assured. We did not share the American estimates, and the lack of discussion on this sensitive topic suggested that the full consequences of a Soviet retaliation had either been miscalculated or, worse, had been deliberately overlooked.

While in Washington I had stayed with an old friend, General Sir Michael West, then the British representative to the Combined Chiefs of Staff. He had known John McCone, the US Director of Central Intelligence, since they had both collaborated in the planning of the

D-Day invasion in 1944. McCone was altogether less sanguine about the likely outcome of a military confrontation than the Pentagon, and he had shared his concerns discreetly with his British friends.

West, who had been in command of the British contingent during the Korean War, was an engaging host, greatly respected by the Americans because his challenges to the Supreme Commander, General Dwight D. Eisenhower, during the invasion planning, had proved prescient. Of course, at the time Eisenhower had not seen West's interventions in quite that way, but the latter had invariably been proved correct. He was an experienced professional, whereas Eisenhower was a political appointee who had never seen combat before D-Day during his lengthy military career. Thus in October 1962 West found himself acting as a conduit during one of the most sensitive periods in Anglo-American relations, adding a valuable understanding of US strategic and tactical thinking. It was a judgement he was uniquely qualified to make.

West was later immortalised by Anthony Powell in his panoramic cycle of novels, *A Dance to the Music of Time*, as the eccentric General Liddament. Characteristically Mike never troubled to read them. He was a great aficionado of pop music, which he played constantly, and at full volume. When a new ADC asked Lady West if she could get the General to turn down the noise, she replied that she had been trying for thirty years.

West's father-in-law was Gus Oppenheim, who had married one of the six Miss Moretons who owned most of Bembridge. When he had become engaged his batman had asked whether the name was Oppenheim or Oppenheimer (of diamond mining fame). When told, he exclaimed, 'Oh, bad luck, Sir!'

While in Washington I had called on the Secretary of State, Dean Rusk, and we relived some of our earlier, wartime experiences, and he told me he was particularly proud of the Silver Star he had been awarded for his work in South-East Asia Command. I also met the US Secretary for Civil Aviation, and when he learned that I was a friend of his counterpart, Julian Amery, he entrusted me with a message for him too secret to be committed to paper. He revealed that the American project to develop a supersonic airliner was proving uneconomic, and he suggested that the British government announce the cancellation of Concorde simultaneously, leaving the Russians to waste vast amounts of money and effort on an entirely fruitless goal. Dutifully, upon my return to London, I conveyed the message to Julian, but he dismissed the idea. Concorde proved a huge success, even if it added to the national debt, and was never allowed to fly across the United States, a route that would have made it much more viable commercially. The American project was duly cancelled and the Soviet Tupolov prototype, nicknamed the Concordski, later crashed very publicly during a demonstration flight at the Paris Air Show.

I was aware of how narrowly a nuclear conflict with Russia had been averted during the Cuban missile crisis. The episode had served to increase Cold War hostility, even if the focus shifted to Germany, where our troops were vastly outnumbered by those of the Warsaw Pact. The strategic analysts believed that any future war would begin either at sea, perhaps by mistake, or in Europe in a surprise attack launched under the guise of a military exercise. Naturally, we had detailed plans prepared for both eventualities, but secrecy was also a key component of our response to aggression. Would we launch a tactical nuclear strike in Germany to delay a Soviet advance to the Channel ports? Did we have nuclear landmines to detonate as the enemy tanks rolled through NATO's inadequate defences along the Rhine? The Allied response depended in large measure on deterring Moscow's hotheads and persuading them that any military advantage would be achieved at appalling cost, but the precise nature of our plans had to remain secret.

The political temperature rose perceptibly after the Cuban crisis, and just when we should have been concentrating on measures to ease tension we were overtaken by a series of extraordinary events that would influence Britain's political life for years to come.

11

Prelude to the Profumo Affair

In retrospect, given my ringside role in what became known as the Profumo affair, I think its origins can be traced back to the machinations of George Wigg, a former wartime lieutenant-colonel in the Education Corps who had represented himself to the Labour Party as a great expert on army matters. He always participated in the army debates and in 1962, when Iraq threatened to invade Kuwait, Wigg advised the Labour Party that Britain would be powerless to honour its defence treaty and mount an effective defence of the tiny, oil-rich, pro-British Gulf state. Being in Opposition, he was unaware of the detailed contingency plans that had been drawn up at the War Office, and knew nothing of the strategy of deterrence that had been adopted by the Cabinet. Both infantry and artillery were flown into Kuwait from Bahrain, and a squadron of tanks had been shipped from Aden, bolstered by an airborne brigade sent direct from Britain. These measures proved effective, and achieved the desired result in Baghdad, where the general staff hurriedly decided against an invasion.

All continued to go well, but unfortunately two clueless servicemen in a truck ignored signs to keep away from the frontier and drove straight into Iraq, where they were arrested and accused of spying, prompting the inevitable Parliamentary Questions. My task, as Jack's PPS, was to anticipate the likely supplementary questions that would follow the main Question: I expected that the worst would be something like, 'How well were these men trained?' This would be awkward to discuss, because if well trained, what were they doing in Iraq but spying? If poorly trained, why were they sent? So the suggested reply was 'They were trained fit for purpose.' In the event the supplementary asked was, 'What were their orders?' and in reply Jack improvised, 'If they got lost they should return to their units,' but it took George Brown a full two minutes to see the joke.

The success of the Kuwait operation left George Wigg looking foolish as his predictions had not been realised. On the contrary, the War Office had taken the crisis in its stride, and had deterred aggression with considerable professionalism. Nevertheless, Wigg demanded a debate, to insist that although the army had reached Kuwait just in time, it would not have been able to mount an effective defence against an Iraqi invasion. This left Jack an opportunity to be conciliatory to Wigg, and he agreed to a debate in which the latter might have his say, but instead the wretched Opposition backbencher was comprehensively savaged by Jack's junior minister, James Ramsden.

Wigg's technique had been to ingratiate himself with ministers by offering them excellent racing tips, and he believed he was very popular, although he was the only person who thought this. Nevertheless, he had received a leaked medical report revealing some dehydration among the troops despatched from England, and he had attempted to use this document to show that the men were unfit for combat. Ramsden contradicted Wigg on every point, making him look like a bad loser, thereby leaving Wigg convinced he had been let down badly by Jack.

Although we had regarded this as one of the occupational hazards of politics, where personalities are bruised in the rough-and-tumble of Parliamentary debate, Jack and I were unaware that these minor victories had been achieved at a price that would be exacted later. Almost simultaneously, there was another, apparently unconnected drama being played out in Whitehall, which would also contribute to the furore that would overwhelm him.

We at the War Office were mere spectators when a spy was discovered in the Admiralty. A relatively junior civil servant, John Vassall, had been passing naval secrets to the Russian KGB, and had been arrested after a surveillance operation following a tip from the CIA. A defector had told the Americans that some years earlier the KGB had recruited a source in Moscow who had continued to compromise classified information following his posting to the Admiralty. Vassall, it emerged, had been blackmailed after he had been caught in a male honey-trap while serving as the British naval attaché's secretary in Moscow.

Under normal circumstances such an episode would have been of only passing interest, but Vassall was an obvious homosexual who had at least attempted to ingratiate himself with an Admiralty minister, Tam Galbraith. In fact Galbraith, as Civil Lord, had merely been acquainted with Vassall, a clerk in his private office who had volunteered to travel up to Scotland to deliver important files to him at his country home, Barskimming in Ayrshire. Vassall had undertaken the task of delivering 'the Admiralty bag' six times, and Galbraith had written a personal note of thanks to Vassall for his help. This entirely innocent letter addressed to 'My dear Vassall' had been used to imply that some improper relationship had existed between the minister and the clerk. None had, but a total of twenty-three letters and postcards, may of them brief and businesslike, written to Vassall by Galbraith were sold to the *Sunday Pictorial*, which prompted George Brown to suggest, under the protection of Parliamentary privilege in the Commons, that further inquiries should be made.

In November 1962 the horrified Galbraith had offered his resignation to Macmillan, who unwisely accepted it, and the episode had set tongues wagging in Westminster. How could Vassall have afforded to live in Dolphin Square on his low pay? How had he slipped through the vetting procedures intended to prevent vulnerable characters from gaining access to classified information? When another minister, Ian Orr-Ewing, later tried to resign so that he could make some money in the City, Macmillan refused to allow him to go for fear that his departure from his government would be misinterpreted.

The Vassall affair really had no political implications, but the government agreed to appoint a committee of inquiry because it had followed so quickly on another, unconnected lapse of security in the Royal Navy, at the Underwater Weapons Research Establishment at Portland in Dorset. On that occasion a former naval petty officer had been blackmailed into collaborating with the KGB while working at the British Embassy in Warsaw, after engaging in the lucrative black market there. Caught in an illegal act, Harry Houghton had agreed to spy for the Russians, and had continued after he had been posted back to England, as a clerk at the sensitive naval base at Portland.

Once again, MI5 had been alerted to Houghton's espionage by the Americans, who had been tipped off by a well-informed defector. Houghton had been placed under surveillance that implicated his girlfriend, Ethel Gee, and had led the watchers to his Soviet contact, an illegal agent, being an intelligence professional operating outside diplomatic immunity, who had adopted the alias of a dead Canadian, Gordon Lonsdale. All had been rounded up in January 1961 in the act of handling stolen documents and sentenced to long terms of imprisonment, and there the matter would have rested if Vassall had not been exposed a year later. Of real concern was the allegation, which proved to be utterly baseless, that the Security Service had bungled the investigation of Houghton and had failed to pursue a clue that would have identified Vassall immediately. According to Percy Hoskins, crime correspondent of the *Daily Express*, the authorities had overlooked evidence of another spy in the Admiralty for eighteen months, following the discovery of a tiny 'microdot' concealed message in the Portland case which had supposedly proved the existence of another, as yet unknown, traitor. In fact, no such microdot ever existed.

The claim had been made by Hoskins and another journalist, Brendan Mulholland, who had simply misjudged the chronology of events and assumed a link between the two different cases. Instead of reporting it as speculation, however, the newspapers had insisted the allegation was based on good information from confidential sources that had to be protected. Of course, there were no such sources and the newsmen had embroidered a tale that doubtless had been further burnished by sub-editors. Whatever the explanation, MI5 assured the Home Secretary that there was absolutely no connection between the two investigations, and nothing had emerged during their pursuit of Houghton in Dorset to suggest the existence of another traitor at the Admiralty in London. Accordingly, the tribunal chaired by Lord Radcliffe challenged the two journalists to name their sources and, when they refused, had Hoskins and Mulholland imprisoned for contempt.

Always reluctant to admit that Fleet Street might be guilty of sheer invention, the editors went on the warpath against the Macmillan administration. This is not to suggest that the Profumo affair was merely a plaything of the press, but it does explain the atmosphere of mutual distrust that existed at the time. George Wigg, exposed as a charlatan, was determined to get his revenge on Profumo; Fleet Street, bruised from the incarceration of two noble defenders of truth, was bent on a counter-attack; and the politicians were conscious that the Prime

Minister had made no effort to protect Tam Galbraith from completely unjustified rumours of a homosexual affair with Vassall.

Tory backbenchers were warned to be very careful in their behaviour and doubtless most understood that neither Macmillan nor the press would tolerate anything that might embarrass his government. As we were later to learn from the inquiry conducted by Lord Denning into some of the wilder stories in circulation about the sexual misconduct of some ministers, not all the members of the Cabinet had entirely heeded the warnings. However, it was beyond credibility that even after Tam's unnecessary resignation had been accepted by Macmillan, another minister could have got himself photographed engaging in oral sex with Margaret, Duchess of Argyle. But that was the widespread belief after the Duke offered the offending pictures as evidence in a sensational divorce case. The Duchess had taken the Polaroid picture herself but it did not include the offender's face, thereby precipitating a plethora of salacious speculation as to the true identity of 'the headless man' (whose identity was never known to the Duke). Although Lord Denning was able, with what physical evidence remained available for scrutiny in the picture, to clear my friend Duncan Sandys of any involvement, the speculation about a minister persisted. Who was the headless man? If not Sandys, was it another minister? These were the questions posed by the press. In political circles however the finger of suspicion was pointed at the former matinee idol Douglas Fairbanks Jnr. Thereafter the newspapers became obsessed with sexual misconduct in high places, and in an era when deference was diminishing, the establishment could no longer expect to escape the media's scrutiny.

12

The Profumo Affair

At the beginning of 1961 the Security Service, MI5, considered a plan to entrap Captain Eugene Ivanov, the Soviet assistant naval attaché at the London embassy. Ivanov had been selected by the Security Service as a likely candidate for coercion or compromise because he was fond of the high life in London to which the society osteopath Stephen Ward had introduced him. He was married to an austere woman whose father was a member of the Supreme Soviet. According to one of his acquaintances who was co-operating with the Secret Intelligence Service and the CIA, Ivanov liked to drink, was attracted to pretty girls and might be susceptible to the right approach. An MI5 case officer was assigned to research how to reach Ivanov when he was most vulnerable, and made a recruitment pitch to Ward over lunch. Afterwards the officer had met the nineteen-year-old Christine Keeler, whom he later described as 'the most beautiful girl I had ever seen'. She was living in Ward's mews house, where Ivanov had been logged as a regular visitor.

A skilled osteopath and a talented amateur artist, and socially ambitious, Ward had encouraged men of distinction into his circle by providing them with call-girls. He had been rented a Thames-side cottage by Lord Astor on his estate at Cliveden near Taplow in Berkshire. When Ward spent weekends at Spring Cottage, he was often accompanied by some of his girls, and this led to a notorious encounter, which was to have serious consequences.

In July 1961 Jack had been Lord Astor's weekend guest at Cliveden, and Ward brought Keeler up from his cottage for a late-night – and costumeless – swim in the pool. At the unscheduled encounter Jack had been dazzled by Christine. Over the next few weeks they planned various assignations, some of them at Ward's mews house. Their affair remained a closely guarded secret, which certainly was not confided to me, and was unknown to the supposedly ubiquitous MI5.

The Security Service, on the other hand, was interested only in gaining access to Ivanov, and surveillance on him had revealed his friendship with Stephen Ward. The decision was taken to recruit Ward in an effort to entrap Ivanov. As Ward appeared to be a friend of Jack's, MI5 took the perfectly sensible precaution of seeking contact with the Secretary of State for War to see if he would be willing to bolster Ward's confidence. The task of approaching a secretary of state fell on the Cabinet Secretary, Sir Norman Brook. In early August 1961 he met Jack, but when he murmured MI5's interest in Ward, and their desire to engage his help in reaching Ivanov, Jack took fright, believing wrongly that Britain's most senior civil servant was delivering a coded warning to steer clear of both Christine and Ward. As Brook, with characteristic diffidence, relayed MI5's request for his co-operation, Jack interpreted this approach as a none-too-subtle hint that MI5, the Cabinet Secretary and the Prime Minister knew he had become involved with Keeler, and that he should end the relationship immediately.

That is precisely what he did, when he wrote a brief note to her on his official letter heading to explain that he could not see her again. Brook, meanwhile, interpreted Jack's reaction as an indignant refusal to be drawn into the sordid business of espionage and passed on a message of refusal to MI5. In fact, of course, Brook had never mentioned Keeler's name, and MI5 were then completely unaware of her existence. Thus both sides thought they had a clear impression of the exchange that had taken place, whereas each was entirely mistaken. Jack was convinced he had received a definite if oblique signal to drop Christine, while MI5 thought the minister had declined to sully himself with the recruitment of a Soviet spy.

Instead of arranging a new assignation with his lover Jack came down to stay with us in Bembridge, where Valerie, her son Mark Havelock-Allen by her first marriage to the film producer, and David Profumo, her son with Jack, had already arrived. My recollection of that weekend on the Isle of Wight is that Jack was unusually subdued, but he definitely did not reveal his unnerving encounter with the Cabinet Secretary. MI5 eventually abandoned their scheme to entrap Ivanov, judging Ward too unreliable to be trusted.

There the matter rested for eighteen months, until Christine Keeler came to the attention of Fleet Street in the beginning of 1963, and learnt the value of kiss-and-tell. She had found herself in difficulties following an unwise relationship with a Jamaican gangster who had been charged with firing a revolver at Ward's front door. He too had been entranced by Christine's breathtaking figure and had pursued her rather too ardently. Reluctant to give evidence against him, she had fled to Spain for the duration of his trial, forcing the prosecution to initiate a search for her. Naturally, the story of the disappearing witness was too tempting for Fleet Street to overlook, especially when Christine, short of money and in fear of her life, claimed to have a sensational tale to reveal.

Although the only supporting evidence of her claim to have shared a passionate affair with Jack was his letter dated August 1961, her colourful version of events was printed by a German and an Italian magazine. Both believed they were immune from Britain's libel laws, but Jack's solicitors brought an action for defamation against them on the grounds that newsstands in London had sold copies of the offending editions. With no more proof than Christine's increasingly hysterical account, backed by the letter, which at best was only mildly incriminating and certainly did not amount to smoking-gun evidence of an affair, Jack extracted apologies in the High Court and damages from both journals.

He also offered his resignation to the Prime Minister, confident that Macmillan had been informed by MI5 at the time of the true nature of his dalliance with Christine. Here, of course, he was completely mistaken. Back in August 1961, when the Cabinet Secretary had made his pitch at MI5's request, nobody in the Security Service had been aware of the affair, which was still developing, and was scarcely six weeks old. It was only much later, after MI5 had concluded that Ward was too unreliable to entrust with such a sensitive assignment, and the police had launched an investigation into Christine's Jamaican boy-friend, that MI5 learned that Jack had been implicated in an affair. At the time, however, the decision had been taken at a senior level within MI5 to ignore the matter as a minister's morals were judged of no concern to the organisation unless there were some security implications, and everyone, or almost everyone, seemed satisfied that this was emphatically not the case in this instance.

Once Jack's offer to resign had been rejected by the Prime Minister, the former assumed that this was tantamount to an instruction to brazen the matter out. As Macmillan saw the situation, Jack's meetings with Ivanov had been entirely social, and could hardly be interpreted as grounds for resignation. The Prime Minister believed that, following the criticism he had received over his immediate acceptance of Galbraith's resignation, he had no proper interest in his minister's private life. Unfortunately, these were matters that nobody felt comfortable in discussing directly with Macmillan because of unique circumstances. The Prime Minister was a cuckold, his Parliamentary colleague Lord Boothby being Lady Dorothy's lover, and the father of her daughter, Sarah Macmillan. Quite what Harold Macmillan thought about this arrangement is anyone's guess, as he never confided his feelings.

Thus, when Jack finally told his friends, myself included, that he had met Keeler briefly in 1961, but that there was no more to it, the story sounded like just another example of press entrapment. Unfortunately, George Wigg saw an opportunity to raise the whole issue, and intended to relate Keeler's story under the protection of Parliamentary privilege. On the Tuesday of that week I warned Jack of Wigg's plan, and asked if I could deny Wigg's version immediately. Jack's response was that any denial would have to come at a much higher level, so I stayed away from Thursday's debate, which duly prompted a crisis. The Chief Whip, Martin Redmayne, and the Attorney-General, Sir John Hobson, summoned Jack back to the Commons after midnight to draft a personal statement to be delivered on Friday morning. Having taken a couple of sleeping pills, Jack was not at his best when he attended this emergency meeting, and presumed that all present in the Chief Whip's room at the Commons knew the Prime Minister's personal position on what had really happened. Still convinced that Macmillan obviously wanted him to face down the story, Jack acquiesced when he was presented with the final draft of the statement, which contained the fatal, and false, assertion that there had been 'no impropriety' in his relationship with Christine Keeler.

From Jack's viewpoint, this was indeed the case. Certainly their affair had been adulterous, but both were consenting adults and, he reasoned, everyone told white lies about extra-marital relationships. This was of no concern to the government, should not have had any impact on his performance as a minister, and was thus an entirely private matter. If Jack had harboured any doubts about this, the Prime Minister had given him the lead. It was inconceivable to Jack, after his stilted interview with the Cabinet Secretary, that Macmillan was unaware of the affair. Surely there could be no other explanation for the warning relayed from MI5? More importantly, there were no security implications to the affair, and Keeler's subsequent claim that Jack's pillow-talk had included a discussion about the deployment of nuclear weapons in West Germany was ludicrous (as Lord Denning rightly concluded when he looked into the issue later).

Jack's confidence was bolstered the next morning when, with Macmillan sitting beside him, he read the statement prepared for him during the early hours. As was usual on a Friday morning, the chamber was far from full, and the Prime Minister's presence was symbolic of his total support. Jack's denial seemed emphatic, and afterwards we shared a bottle of champagne in his room while he changed to attend Sandown races with the Queen Mother. All seemed well, and the storm clouds had parted as quickly as they had gathered. Or so it seemed.

The issue of misleading the Commons is considered by outsiders to be heinous, but actually Chancellors are often obliged to give misleading replies to protect the country's economy. To offer entirely honest and straightforward answers to questions on the value of the pound, or the Treasury's intention to devalue the currency, or restrict the Sterling Area, would be economic suicide. It would have been hard to find anyone who really believed Selwyn Lloyd when he had assured the Commons that there had been 'no collusion' with the Israelis prior to the invasion of Egypt during the 1956 Suez crisis. Far from ending his political career, Selwyn had been elected Speaker after this flat lie in the chamber, and he was never criticised for it.

In Jack's case, he had felt an obligation and loyalty to the Prime Minister, still convinced that Macmillan knew the real circumstances, and thought his misleading statement had been part of the strategy. At the Whitsun break when Jack took Valerie to Venice, however, he admitted the truth to her and she, furious, insisted that he return to London at once to confess and resign. To reflect upon the situation he went into hiding for a time at a friend's country house in Warwickshire, and even though reporters were offering huge sums to reveal his whereabouts, the staff stayed loyal and Jack evaded the press. His position was now impossible and he concluded that the only honourable course was to tender his resignation: this he now did by way of a letter to the Prime Minister preceded by a call to his PPS. It is not true, as has been suggested, that Jack was deprived of membership of the Privy Council. He discussed it with me at this time and decided to resign from it himself. Naturally, when Jack resigned office, I remained a loyal supporter, and did what I could to help him.

A full-scale debate on the affair was held in the Commons in June, and William Shepherd, a Tory MP, claimed he had seen what he termed 'the four principal parties' in a nightclub together in November 1961. This was a shocking disclosure, and completely at odds with what Jack had now told me. Accordingly, when Shepherd left the chamber I raced after him and asked him who his four were. He replied, 'Ward, Ivanov, Keeler and Rice-Davies'. This was a great relief, and I explained that he had given the impression that Profumo had been there too, as one of 'the four principal parties', so he promised to correct this later in the debate.

This seemingly small incident was to have much wider consequences because, in his wind-up speech, George Brown said that it was clear that Profumo had continued to see Keeler months after his supposed warning-off in August. I looked for Shepherd to intervene to correct this misapprehension, but he did not, and so the Commons was left with the damaging and erroneous impression that Jack had recklessly disregarded the advice given to him by the Cabinet Secretary. The truth, of course, was that Jack had been so struck by the warning that he had written immediately to Keeler, and never saw her again. Nevertheless, yet another Profumo myth had been created, and this one entirely by accident, or at least by Shepherd's omission.

The debate was an ordeal for Jack's friends, and it was painful to hear Nigel Birch insist that a three-line whip was a summons to attend, and could not be an order on how to vote, especially on an issue such as this. In the subsequent division the government's majority fell dramatically, and Macmillan was thought to be hopelessly out of touch. Could it really be true that MI5 had not informed him of what his ministers were up to?

The explanation for this apparent lapse would not emerge for years, and certainly after the resignations of Lords Jellicoe and Lambton, both ministers in Ted Heath's administration who would regularly use the services of a well-known prostitute, Norma Levy, whose husband was an informant for Scotland Yard. Neither George Jellicoe nor Tony Lambton was renowned for his fidelity, and George had been appointed by Harold Macmillan after the Queen had inquired in 1962 why he was not a minister. Macmillan had explained that George had a Catholic wife who would not grant him a divorce, so he was living in sin with another woman. Apparently the Queen had remarked that she had no rooted objection, so George had been made a minister, and evidently believed he had a royal licence to sin.

The Security Service had always taken the view that their remit had never extended to policing the morals of ministers, and provided there were no security implications, how they conducted themselves was a matter for the whips and not for MI5. The secrecy surrounding the organisation meant that few outsiders really understood its true role, and the Director-General took great care not to transgress the traditional limits of his authority. Of course, there had been numerous opportunities to convey a hint that all was not well. The Director-General's own brother was a Tory MP, and the Deputy Director-General, Graham Mitchell, was known to me as a neighbour in Bembridge who sailed club boats, as I did, throughout August. Indeed, he had worked at Central Office's research department before the war. It certainly did not occur to me, however, to ask Mitchell for some off-the-record guidance, and it would have been quite improper for him to have given it.

Only years later did I learn of the sub-currents flowing at the time that had influenced some of these events. Although the two journalists had invented their tale about a link between Vassall and the Portland spies, MI5 had been concerned about the possibility of yet another traitor in the Admiralty. The suspect had been a much more senior figure, who was later to rise to the rank of admiral, and the assertion that the original investigation of Houghton had been bungled had struck a very sensitive nerve within the tiny group of officers who knew the full picture. They had been anxious to find out whether the reporters had simply manufactured the story, or whether there was indeed a definite lead behind the claim, which might implicate the suspect naval officer. In the event the whole matter was written off as a newspaper fabrication, and the investigation into further breaches of security at the Admiralty quietly shelved.

Another hidden component in the chronicle was Mitchell himself, who had acted as the principal conduit of information between MI5 and the Prime Minister's office. The public would learn only in 1981 that the Deputy Director-General was also, at that very moment, the subject of a mole hunt and suspected of passing secrets to the KGB. Incredibly, when Mitchell had walked from his office at Leconfield House in Curzon Street, to brief the PM's private secretary, then temporarily accommodated at Admiralty House in Whitehall while 10 Downing Street was being renovated, he had been followed by a team of watchers convinced he could be going to meet a Soviet contact. Little wonder that the Director-General, Sir Roger Hollis, was less than enthusiastic about giving the Prime Minister comprehensive reports on what was happening in his government with the risk of drawing his own service into the spotlight.

The pain of the saga was extended by the appointment of the Master of the Rolls, Lord Denning, to look into what precisely had happened, and his report duly became a best-seller. He revealed, for the first time, the directive issued by Sir David Maxwell-Fyfe, the Home Secretary in 1951 who had strictly limited the role of the Security Service, and explained the organisation's unique, semi-independent role in White-hall, which prevented MI5 officers from snooping into the private lives of government ministers.

Denning took evidence from all quarters, with the exception of Stephen Ward, by this time dead, and even looked into some of the other rumours that had circulated in Westminster, including the now-notorious 'headless man' and 'the man in the mask', both alleged to have been members of the Cabinet. The latter had supposedly attended louche Mayfair parties dressed only in a mask and small apron. Needless to say no ministerial connection was discovered.

At MI5's request Denning had passed lightly over the precise nature of the organisation's interest in Ivanov, who had fled the country long since, but had drawn an unflattering picture of Bill Astor's circle of friends.

The Profumo affair was a tragedy for almost all concerned. Jack withdrew from public affairs, devoting the remainder of his life to charitable activities. He worked for, and later ran, Toynbee Hall, an East End establishment where the qualification for joining the boys' club is to have been thrown out of two other boys' clubs. The boys respected

Jack because as one put it, 'if he could pull a bird like Keeler he must be one hell of a guy'.

Jack gave many years' service to the charity and was rewarded with a CBE in 1975, and with the renewed friendship of the Royal Family. He sat next to the Queen at a private dinner at Claridge's to mark Mrs Thatcher's seventieth birthday. He was also supported by Valerie, who stood by him with great courage and was much admired for her loyalty. He died in March 2006 aged ninety-one.

Stephen Ward, facing a criminal charge of living off immoral earnings, took a drug overdose and died in hospital. His defence had been that he was working for MI5, but his case officer had been using an alias, and the telephone number was disconnected. He was unaware that his MI5 case officer had pleaded with Sir Roger Hollis to allow evidence to be given on his behalf. With nothing to support his apparently wild claims of working for British Intelligence, Ward was ruined. George Wigg was given a Wilson peerage and was arrested several times for kerb-crawling after prostitutes.

As for myself, I felt terribly for Jack and his family, but knew the cause had been lost, but not entirely for the reasons the public and the media believed. If only Jack had grasped the real import of the Cabinet Secretary's intervention in July 1961, and if only the Cabinet Secretary had spoken in plain English and had made his position clear, the political and social history of the 1960s might have been altered. As it was, Britain's most senior civil servant had evidently felt some distaste at his role as an intermediary for MI5 and had failed to spell out precisely the nature of the organisation's request, leaving Jack to jump to the wrong conclusion.

Although ambitious, Jack was a deeply honourable man who could never be compared with the politicians of more recent times, who cling to office because of ministerial status, perks and pay. In those days almost everyone who entered public life did so at considerable personal financial cost, and Jack had not hesitated to offer his resignation to the Prime Minister at the appropriate moment. He would never have jeopardised security: tales about Keeler pumping him for classified information at Captain Ivanov's instruction are inventions fabricated later to help sell various versions of her memoirs. Characteristically, after having been interviewed by Lord Denning, and earned the judge's respect for the candour of his replies, Jack himself remained silent on the tragedy for the remainder of his life.

Many ministers have had mistresses, even prime ministers, and I often think that if Jack had been allowed to resign and sit on the back-benches it would all soon have been forgotten. Instead, his name has become synonymous with the febrile atmosphere and unpleasantness surrounding the last days of the Macmillan government.

13

Into Opposition

After a short interval James Ramsden, who had been the junior minister in the War Office, was appointed Secretary of State for War, and he asked me to continue as Parliamentary Private Secretary. He was a charming man with a brilliant intellect, but lacked Jack's charisma. Nevertheless, I enjoyed working with him and accompanied him on a tour of the Far East to inspect our bases in Malaysia and Hong Kong. In Sarawak we flew by helicopter to the border with Indonesia where, once again, British troops were deployed to protect the local population from communist-backed insurgents.

The local British commander was General Sir Walter Walker, whom I had known when we had attended Staff College together, and he was conducting a brilliant campaign. He had deployed the SAS deep in the jungle mounting ambushes against the guerrillas, although there was a rule, occasionally obeyed, that the camps on the other side of the border should not be attacked. The tactics adopted, of small patrols working far from their bases, being resupplied by helicopters, proved very effective, although the exact nature of the operations was concealed from the public, and from Parliament. We were taken to one of the forward observation posts, overlooking the frontier, and when the helicopter experienced problems, it looked as though we might have to undertake an eighteen-hour trek through the rainforest to get back. Fortunately the rest of the trip proved uneventful, although on our way to Hong Kong we were buzzed by US Air Force fighters from Vietnam in spite of our aircraft's RAF markings.

On the Wednesday of the Conservative Party conference at Blackpool in October 1963 it was announced that Harold Macmillan intended to retire as Prime Minister, and the search for his successor was under way. Macmillan had been diagnosed with prostate cancer and a doctor had told him that this would be the end of his political career. It was only after he had submitted his resignation to the Queen, while still in hospital, that he was informed that his operation had been a complete success and he could resume his post. By then, of course, it was too late to change his mind, although he told his grandson, Alexander, the present Earl of Stockton, that he wanted to go back to the Queen and withdraw his resignation.

Naturally, the prospect of choosing a new leader, and Prime Minister, transformed the annual conference from a relatively mundane, routine distraction into a maelstrom of political manoeuvring, and there was intense speculation about the succession. On the Wednesday I dined with Earl St Aldwyn, the Conservative Chief Whip in the Lords, before going to a meeting addressed by Viscount Hailsham. At the very end the latter announced his intention to resign his peerage to offer himself as Prime Minister, this to great excitement. He then went on to the Young Conservative ball, where he was received with cheers. After the meeting we went to the conference hotel where Rab Butler joined us for a drink, evidently in great distress. As the deputy Prime Minister, he thought he was Macmillan's obvious successor, but he had been received in silence by those present, in contrast to the rapturous applause that Quentin Hailsham had experienced.

Rab was a brilliant Tory intellectual, and his Education Act, introduced in 1952, must have been a work of genius, especially since every reform since has been disastrous. He had married a Courtauld, and so had enjoyed immense riches, but as Home Secretary he had proved indecisive, always appointing a Royal Commission when any difficult problem came up, thereby postponing a decision. I recalled the party conference in Bournemouth in 1957, when I had attended as a prospective candidate and had been horrified when in his speech Rab had referred to dining on over-ripe pheasant and vintage port, hardly the food of the masses then, and emotive to this day as David Cameron has learned. So, when Anthony Eden had resigned as Prime Minister, I voted against Rab, as I did again in 1963.

The following day, Reggie Maudling, as Chancellor of the Exchequer, made his speech to the conference, and it went down quite well. That evening I said to him, 'I thought you were going to throw your hat in the ring?' He replied, 'Oh dear, didn't I?' I admired Reggie's political wisdom and quick brain. When Jack Profumo took over from him the post of Aviation Minister, Jack inquired if the job required a lot of work. Reggie said that it took him half a morning, but Jack found he needed all day. Reggie had taken a first in Greats at Oxford. I once asked Dick Crossman how it was that in the *Economist* you could always read the definitive article on a subject, knowing that he contributed to the magazine. Crossman loftily replied, 'If you have a first in Greats you can write the definitive article on any subject.'

Many brilliant politicians, Pitt the Younger included, have been unable to organise their private lives. For all his intelligence, Reggie was unable to compete with the demands of his family. Later he would get himself mixed up with two dubious financiers, one in Yorkshire and one in Zurich. It is possible, perhaps, to laugh off one such mistake, but more than that seems to indicate a habit, and Reggie's reputation never recovered.

When, at the end of the most politically significant party conference for decades, I flew back to London, Quintin grinned at me as he took the seat in front. Then I noticed Randolph Churchill slide over to sit beside him, and together they discussed the changes to be made at Downing Street. No one had considered the Earl of Home as a candidate at that stage, and it was clear that both Quintin and Randolph believed they knew who would be summoned to the Palace to form a new Conservative administration. They would both be proved wrong.

I had always admired Alec Home, and when he was Foreign Secretary I had asked him why we were taking no action in the Yemeni war. I had some knowledge of the region because a friend and Parliamentary colleague, Billy McLean, was fighting on the royalist side against the communists. In conversation with Alec I suggested British help against the communists was desirable, but he replied, 'Have you considered where British interests lie? The only threat to Aden is the Yemen and so long as Yemen is otherwise occupied, so much the better.'

This was a rather Machiavellian approach, but I was delighted to hear that the Foreign Office even considered British interests. My experience had been that Foreign Office diplomats often seemed more intent on appeasing our adversaries.

Alec, the compromise choice for the leadership, was popular on the Tory benches in the Commons, but his natural charm, good manners and honesty proved insufficiently telegenic in an affluent era in which television exercised increasing influence in the election campaign. He was lampooned for taking to the grouse moors.

The Conservatives lost at the General Election of 1964, and Harold Wilson became prime minister. When we went into Opposition I decided to concentrate on housing and local government, of which I had some experience. Having served on Kensington Council I had come to understand the economics of housing and the needs of tenants. John Boyd-Carpenter was appointed the Shadow minister, and therefore chairman of the back-bench committee. I was elected one of his two vice-chairmen, and continued to hold that post until 1970. So for six years I was an Opposition front-bench spokesman on housing, which was to prove a key political issue.

After thirteen years as a minister, Boyd-Carpenter, despite a brilliant brain, had become rather staid. He had been used to having his speeches written for him by civil servants and lacked the imagination or dynamism to develop the new policies we needed to appeal to an increasingly affluent electorate. As he was not particularly expert on housing, which had never been his portfolio in government, he left a lot of routine Opposition work to his subordinates, myself among them.

When replaced as Shadow minister by Geoffrey Rippon, the latter gladly maintained the custom, having a busy practice at the Bar. Luckily at the Conservative Research Department John McGregor, later a Cabinet minister, dealt with housing and proved an excellent speechwriter, but was soon poached by Ted Heath. As a team we proved effective, however, and we were able to demonstrate the depth of our knowledge when the Labour Government produced some ill-considered proposals; we were able to subject them to detailed scrutiny. When the Land Commission Bill was considered for a record 120 hours in committee, and a record 20 hours at report stage on the floor of the House, Geoffrey made no appearance, leaving everything to Graham Page and myself on the Opposition front-bench.

Later, the ambitious Peter Walker was appointed and our rather successful team was changed. He engaged outside advisers to help with policy and froze out his Parliamentary colleagues. He did, however, have the sense to adopt my proposals for 'right to buy' for tenants of public authority housing. This was a policy I had developed directly as a result of my contact with tenants of the New Towns Commission in my own constituency, and with the local authority. When first elected

I had made it a practice to call on constituents at random to find out their problems. I was particularly struck by one lady who told me that she wished to own her house instead of renting it. I suggested that there were plenty of houses for sale in the area, but she was adamant that she wanted this particular house, having dug the garden and fitted the carpets. I said, 'I think you have a point,' and began advocating 'the right to buy'. Strong opposition came from the vested interests of housing managers, but I worked on over the years until I convinced my fellow Tories, and eventually even the Labour Party.

It made perfect sense to me that a tenant should be allowed to acquire ownership of his or her own home, and when the economics were examined one could see that the average local authority tenant remaining in the same property for many years probably paid the original cost several times over, but died without owning a brick of it. Where was the justice in such a system that discriminated against tenants who paid rent, yet offered tax incentives to anyone with a mortgage? Even the argument that local authorities should have a stock of public housing available to house people at the lower end of the income scale did not really undermine my proposals, as the statistics demonstrated that a tenant tended to stay put for decades. This was also an obstacle to the movement of labour, so essential if an economy was going to respond to local or regional demands. The 'right to buy' had the added advantage that it was likely to prove attractive to voters who might not otherwise be expected to vote Conservative. Accordingly it eventually made its way into the 1970 election manifesto, and was judged to have been a factor in our success in the General Election.

On another constituency visit, I called on one John de Borse, who had a strange story to tell. Two years earlier, his body had been riddled with cancer and he was given only days to live. As a devout Catholic, he wished to visit Lourdes, but no airline would take him because of the risk of his dying on board, so Group Captain Leonard Cheshire flew him there. After admission at the hospital, he was carried to the grotto on a stretcher. On arrival, he felt a profound change. Dismissing his stretcher-bearers, de Borse walked the three miles back to the hospital. On the way he felt hungry and had a meal in a restaurant, the first proper one for three weeks. He admitted that he felt a bit tired for the next two days, but thereafter was fine. Back in London, his new X-rays simply did not match the old ones: the cancer had vanished. I kept in touch with him for the next ten years, getting him jobs which he could not keep for long because of a violent temper. I visited him in St Joseph's Hospice in the East End the night before he died.

In the 1959 Parliament, I found I had some delightful colleagues, among them Clive Bossom, Philip Goodhart, Harwood Harrison and Peter Roberts, with whom I have never had a cross word. But one or two others were less pleasant. I was astonished at the opening words of the maiden speech of Humphrey Berkeley. 'It is an honour to make one's maiden speech in this Chamber, but an even greater one to make it immediately after that of one's dearest friend'. Peter Tapsel, with whom he shared a flat, must have been intensely embarrassed at the construction that the press might have put on that: professions of homosexuality were unusual at the time, certainly among politicians. Berkeley irritated me by constantly drawing attention to himself by criticising the government. So when the new Tory back-benchers had a meeting with the Chief Whip, I suggested that we should all get a ration of acts of disloyalty with its attendant publicity, instead of Berkeley hogging it all. He glowered at me.

When Alec Home became Prime Minister, it was the self-promoting Berkeley who demanded a change in the method of selecting the leader. He lost his seat in the 1964 election and took a job with a charity where he and Jeffrey Archer became mixed up in a financial mess, with each blaming the other. Soon afterwards Archer won a by-election, so I greeted him with the words, 'Any enemy of Humphrey Berkeley is a friend of mine.' But I soon discovered how bogus Archer was, and did not pursue my offer of friendship.

After a year in Opposition in 1965, Alec Home resigned, and we had to find a new leader. The procedure had hitherto been mysterious. When Bonar Law was taken seriously ill, his private secretary, John Davidson, still in his twenties, had taken it upon himself to write to King George V to say that in this modern democracy, when even women had the vote, it was essential the Prime Minister should be an elected member of the Commons. The King naturally thought this was Bonar Law's advice, which it was not. So Baldwin became Prime Minister in place of the much better qualified Lord Curzon. It was a coincidence that Baldwin and Davidson afterwards became the best of friends.

Subsequent leadership changes were undisputed until the resignation of Eden, when the choice lay between Macmillan and Butler. As a

Parliamentary candidate I was consulted in what was perhaps a secret ballot. When it came to choosing Macmillan's successor, I voted for Maudling. I was then asked, 'If you can't have him, will you agree to Alec Home?'' I assented. But now the system had become more transparent. The choice was by open ballot of MPs only, because they best understood the abilities of the contestants. Heath, with his whip's experience, knew that a personal approach to every vote was essential. Maudling took the view that MPs could well make up their own minds. Heath, the practical man, won over the better brains of Maudling and Powell.

When Ted became leader, the *Daily Express* commissioned a study of his image with the public. He played the organ and messed about in dinghies wearing shorts, so he gave the impression of a wet scout master. To toughen up his image, he should, it was suggested, take up ocean racing, wear oilies and smoke a pipe. When shown this, Ted was furious but nevertheless followed the advice – except for the pipe. Our colleague, Dick Sharples, an experienced sailor, advised Ted against moving straight from dinghies to an ocean racer, but Ted was nothing if not determined.

His first test in his yacht *Morning Cloud* was the Round the Island race in 1968. I was with Admiral Morgan Morgan-Giles on his boat. Soon after the start, as the fleet tacked westwards, we sailed close under the stern of *Morning Cloud*, and gave a cheery hail to Ted, at the helm. The hail was not returned; he looked very tense.

Ted appointed Enoch Powell as Shadow Defence Minister. When the Labour Government announced the intention of withdrawing our forces from the Persian Gulf, Enoch seemed unperturbed. I pointed out that we relied on the Gulf for our oil supplies, and our military presence ensured that the sheikhdoms remained friendly. If any sheikh got out of line he found himself replaced by someone more co-operative. Characteristically Enoch replied, 'I can prove you are wrong. Japan gets all the oil they need from the Gulf, and has not a soldier there.' It was characteristic of his mind: brilliant theory occasionally untempered by common sense.

Another friend and a fellow of All Souls, John Foster, was a more successful barrister than politician. He became Minister of State at the Commonwealth Office, in the Eden administration, and one day had to attend Cabinet in the absence of the Secretary of State. There he contradicted the Prime Minister, and although he could see that Eden was losing his temper he would not give way. So he was returned to the back-benches and his legal practice in international law. Here he was so successful that potential litigants paid him an annual retainer to ensure that he did not appear against them. He told me that his secret was to keep one legal point up his sleeve until the final Court of Appeal, where its production left the other side no notice in which to construct a convincing reply.

Foster complained in the 1922 Committee that my lengthy opposition to the Land Commission Bill was making the bill more intelligible, whereas it should be left for the judges to resolve after becoming law. I believed then and now that he was profoundly wrong. All too often we have seen Brussels impose ill-thought-out laws, which are then enthusiastically enforced by British bureaucrats with little regard to common sense.

One winter's day I went with the old Etonian Labour MP Tam Dalyell to visit the Chemical Warfare Research Establishment at Porton Down. He was serving as PPS to Dick Crossman, then Minister for Technology. Porton had been seeking volunteers from the forces to research the common cold. In fact they were to be guinea pigs for research into the effects of anthrax and nerve gases. At our meeting with the commandant Tam asked him why he was researching the common cold, when national research was taking place at the Cavendish Institute at Cambridge. The reply was that this was a part of the Cavendish research. It seemed odd that valuable servicemen should be used to supplement civilians. Had Tam followed this up by checking with the Cavendish he might have uncovered something, unless the Cavendish was part of the conspiracy. Years later, Tam demanded the prosecution of the scientists concerned, and a long police inquiry ensued. But I thought that those who were guilty were the politicians who had authorised the process.

Our poor showing in the 1966 election was a disappointment but hardly unexpected, and gave our new leader, Ted Heath, the opportunity to reshuffle his Shadow Cabinet and bring in some younger men, including Anthony Barber and naturally Peter Walker, the architect of his own victory as leader. Thus the party was unified, and ready for a long stretch in Opposition, which would give it an opportunity to develop new policies intended to sweep Labour from power. The one fly in the ointment was the insoluble problem of Rhodesia, which had made a Unilateral Declaration of Independence (UDI) in November 1965 to avoid the terms under which Britain had required a transfer to black majority rule. Like many on the Conservative benches, led by Lord Salisbury in the Lords, and Major Pat Wall in the Commons, I was sympathetic to the 'kith and kin' who had settled in East Africa and made the country such an economic success. To the exasperation of Willie Whitelaw, the Chief Whip, we could not bring ourselves to vote in favour of sanctions which, as Wilson famously claimed, would bring Ian Smith down in 'weeks not months'.

What troubled me was the obvious decline in the living standards of everyone, especially the indigenous populations, of those countries that had been granted independence. Invariably Macmillan's best intentions had been subverted by corrupt one-party regimes, which had robbed their own people of the opportunities that the now-despised empire had offered them. Of course, UDI had been an extreme step, but who could blame the residents whose families had settled there generations ago and made Rhodesia a prosperous country, rich in agriculture and minerals? What had been accomplished by the farmers had been placed in jeopardy by Soviet-backed Marxist guerrillas, whose plans for land redistribution were so reminiscent of the collectivisation policies that had proved catastrophic elsewhere. The eventual expropriation of the lands farmed by whites would spell ruin for Zimbabwe under Mugabe's corrupt regime.

Like others in the party, I felt one-man one-vote democracy was a fine ultimate objective, but its immediate imposition on a largely rural, relatively unsophisticated population would wreck years of steady investment, stability and development. I instinctively thought of the Kariba Dam, a hugely impressive monument to the commitment made by the colonial authorities to bringing hydro-electric power to far-flung communities north and south of the Zambesi. Why should such achievements be put at risk for short-term political expediency? Surely it was our duty to take the longer view and protect the interests for whom we still retained some responsibility.

When the 1922 Committee, the weekly meeting of back-bench Tory MPs, first discussed UDI, the discussion naturally turned to the practicability of military force to restore sovereignty. I warned that some officers would probably resign their commissions rather than lead their men against the white settlers. The idea spread and it was one of the factors in Wilson's decision against direct intervention. He chose sanctions instead. I took the view that if we had abandoned our claim to sovereignty we should accept the status quo. We have done this in many West African states where there has been a change of government after we relinquished sovereignty. The imposition of sanctions seemed a spiteful attempt to starve an opponent into submission.

The issue would torment the party, as the sanctions order would be renewed every November, creating a continuing embarrassment for the leadership, which was quite unable to bring the hardcore of recalcitrants into line. For Whitelaw and his whips, the options were limited, for those of us who felt most strongly on this subject were virtually immune to the blandishments and threats of the whips, and certainly could not be coerced through constituency pressure when grassroots opinion was overwhelmingly in sympathy with us.

On one occasion, 21 December, the Tories split three ways, with thirty-one supporting the government, fifty against, and the rest, led by the front-bench, abstaining. As Whitelaw later admitted, 'The result was a total disaster for a Chief Whip.'

As a former Chief Whip, Heath probably understood Whitelaw's frustrations better than most, and there was certainly no personal antagonism between those of us who opposed the sanctions orders, and the remainder of the Parliamentary party, which acknowledged our leader's attempt to be expedient. Heath, whose social and persuasive skills were limited, found himself increasingly in conflict with traditional Tories, however. The wreck of Rhodesia served to provide an overt example of the struggle, which was not merely a conventional left–right conflict, but a deep, unacknowledged schism in the party. Exacerbating this tense situation was Heath's dismissal of Ernest Marples, John Boyd-Carpenter and Duncan Sandys, all popular figures sacrificed in a drive to modernise the party. These were not acts calculated to enhance Heath's popularity and I, along with other colleagues, was dismayed at his apparent unwillingness to take the appropriate steps to win over his mounting critics and make new friends.

14

Back into Power

Gambling is forbidden in the Palace of Westminster and when we went into Opposition in 1964, Michael Noble became a director of Associated Fish, a company with an office nearby where we could play bridge undisturbed. In those days the Commons frequently sat on after the ten o'clock vote, and it was not unusual for business to last for several more hours, if not all night, as we attempted to harry the government. Of course, we had to be on hand in case of a vote, ready to respond to the division bell and race to the lobbies in the eight minutes allowed before the Badge Messengers locked the doors.

Bridge was a wonderful way of passing this time, and with Michael as our host, and plenty of smoked salmon courtesy of the company, plus some excellent malt whisky, the hours of what might otherwise have been tedious waiting were a delight, engaged in card playing with congenial companions. What more could an opposition member ask?

When we returned to government in 1970, we started playing bridge in David Gibson-Watt's ministerial room. He had been appointed Under Secretary of State for Wales, and the Serjeant-at-Arms, who heard of our card playing, wisely decreed that bridge was henceforth to be considered a game of skill, and therefore allowed within the precincts of the Palace of Westminster. Our agreeable bridge group contained three who became Cabinet ministers and life peers, Michael Noble, David Gibson-Watt and Kenneth Baker. The regulars also included Tim Kitson, then Ted's PPS. On one occasion Sally Oppenheim offered to drive us home when the House finally rose in the early hours. Kitson asked to be dropped at 10 Downing Street but Sally, wisely anticipating how a press photographer might misconstrue the situation, insisted on depositing him in Whitehall.

After the 1970 Conservative election victory I was elected chairman of the Conservative back-bench housing committee, which met weekly, a post I was to hold for the next four years, and one that kept me in close touch with Julian Amery and Paul Channon, the successive housing ministers. One difficulty was that values of commercial and office property were rising so fast that it became profitable to leave a property empty. Suddenly Tony Barber, the Chancellor, without consulting anyone, produced his own solution. It proved to be a disaster so severe that it led to the collapse of several banks.

Many of the characters then in the House conveyed a distinctly larger-than-life impression. I was present in the chamber when Ian Paisley made his maiden speech. There is a rule that MPs may not move between an MP addressing the House and the Speaker, so as I was seated directly between the Ulsterman and the Speaker, I was obliged to remain seated throughout his speech. After several distinctive 'Mishter Shpeaker Shiirs' I was in need of an umbrella, but had to remain rooted to the bench.

Iain Macleod was an expert bridge player who wrote a book on bidding and had represented Britain at the game, but when he joined White's Club he was mystified by the play. It took him several weeks to discover that everyone else was mystified too. As Minister of Health under Churchill he had announced that the link between smoking and cancer had been proven – while chain smoking throughout the press conference. A powerful liberal thinker and inspiring speaker, particularly at party conferences, he was not an easy man to relate to. Although a close friend of Enoch Powell's of many years' standing, after the latter's 'Rivers of Blood' speech on immigration Macleod never spoke to him again. From principle, doubtless, but it was none the less seen as a failure of the persuasive approach to which Conservatism was dedicated.

During the Heath government, when Macleod was Leader of the House, there was a free vote on whether to allow television cameras into the chamber. When the decision went against the proposal, I proceeded to White's to celebrate and, meeting Macleod as he was leaving, told him the news. A day or two later I read a press interview in which he said that he had not attended the debate because it was a free vote, and he had not needed to be there. Thus it had afforded him an opportunity to spend the evening with his crippled wife.

Willie Whitelaw was in many respects Macleod's polar opposite. His avuncular air and humour carried him effortlessly across divisions within the party. Despite being the best Chief Whip post-war, he would perform no greater service than as Margaret Thatcher's *consigliere* for a decade, persuading and explaining the gameplan to members of the Parliamentary party while conveying to her the limits of the possible. For beneath the oyster-eyed benevolence a shrewd political brain was at work and a degree of ruthlessness that enabled him to sideline rivals. Sometimes it seemed that the opposing aspects of his character fought each other to a standstill. As Home Secretary from 1979 he demoralised his junior ministers by vacillating upon important issues, and came close to allowing himself to be taken prisoner by the self-perpetuating liberal culture installed by Roy Jenkins. This was surprising, for he was not without courage, having won a Military Cross as a tank commander in Normandy during the war. In the event he embarked upon a massive programme of prison building and an expansion of the police force.

It was not a happy time for Willie, with riots in Toxteth and Brixton, and a rising prison population to contend with. He confided to me with a sigh how much he had enjoyed walking unrecognised in his constituency, until he had become Secretary of State for Northern Ireland in 1972. Thereafter he had been on the television night after night and recognised everywhere. Willie's common sense was acclaimed and his premeditated gaffes much enjoyed, as when during the 1970 General Election he accused Harold Wilson of 'going round the country stirring up apathy'. Willie's elevation to the upper chamber as the first hereditary peer for a generation would provide an opportunity for that rarity in politics, a happy ending, as Lord President of the Council and Leader of the House of Lords.

Among the new intake at the 1970 election was a constituent and former BOAC pilot, Norman Tebbit, who looked to me for advice, and promptly found himself appointed secretary to the Housing Committee. I had explained that this kind of donkeywork, undertaken outside the chamber and certainly unnoticed by the public, was much appreciated by the whips. If he was ambitious, as I believed, he could gain preferment and promotion without necessarily attracting a lot of attention by making too many speeches in the Commons. Much of the business of the House is far from glamorous and takes place away from the media. But it is noticed by those who count when a new MP is attempting to build his career. Norman appreciated my help, even if my strictures about politeness from our benches were not always heeded, and he became a firm friend.

While I had little time for class warriors such as Dennis Skinner, I got on well with many members opposite, whom I considered misguided idealists. My military life had given me little experience of trade unions. Norman Tebbit, however, had, as a shop steward at the British Airline Pilots Association, witnessed the abuse of trade unionism from the inside, and became a powerful and effective opponent. He considered all Labour members guilty of supporting a tyrannous system that impoverished those for whom it purported to act.

Another constituent, Cecil Parkinson, soon followed Norman into the Commons at a by-election. Cecil sought my advice when he was invited to become Parliamentary Private Secretary to Michael Heseltine. I pointed to the latter's reputation for arrogance and lack of scruple. Cecil thought he sounded like a politician with a great future – and took the job.

When Margaret Thatcher was considering her first reshuffle in 1981 she invited Norman to be Chairman of the Party. He said he would prefer a department, and that the right man for Chairman was Cecil Parkinson. Margaret asked who he was, and Norman replied, 'One of your Ministers of State.' Cecil proved a great success at Central Office and Norman became Minister of Employment. He would tell the endless delegations of trade unionists who came to protest at his reforms, 'I have been a shop steward myself, so let's agree to leave out that bit about "the lads won't wear it".'

Cecil might not have been particularly familiar to Margaret at that time, but I certainly knew who he was. Years earlier, when I had tried to attend all the annual general meetings of all my constituency branches, I had gone to the Flamstead 1960 village meeting. The secretary, a Mrs Ann Parkinson, had announced the resignation of the treasurer and, in the absence of any other volunteers, had persuaded her husband, Cecil, a chartered accountant, to take the job, his very first in the Tory Party.

A year later my agent had invited Cecil to become chairman of the constituency's political committee and, on asking how many members it had, he was told, 'If you accept, one.' He remembered that a friend of his, an airline pilot, was on strike, so he persuaded Norman Tebbit to become vice-chairman, which was to be his very first job in the Conservative Party. Forty years later, when both men were leaving the House of Lords together, one said to the other, 'Who would have thought then that this is where we should pitch up?'

Cecil had a very similar experience to Jack Profumo's. As ministers, both sinned; both had loyal and forgiving wives. Cecil had to retire as a minister, but only temporarily. In contrast, Robin Cook would abandon his wife and marry his mistress – and still remain in office. Such are the wages of sin.

When at Central Office Cecil introduced Jock Lawson from Berkhamsted as the party's treasurer, and David Smith, my old constituency agent. This combination became known to Margaret Thatcher as 'the Hemel Hempstead mafia' but ensured that Central Office was run with unprecedented efficiency. Lawson had a narrow escape when the Grand Hotel in Brighton was bombed during the party conference. He was called away on that Thursday morning and at lunchtime, when I had a drink with Tony Berry, he told me that he had been fortunate to have been able to take over Lawson's room. I had been in Brighton to protest against allowing forty-four tonne lorries into Britain, and learned the next day that Tony had been killed in the explosion.

When in 1972 there was a vote in the Commons on entry into the European Economic Community, I asked Edward Boyle his view and he advised that it was marginally in Britain's economic interest to join, so I voted in favour. Entry meant we were entitled to send representatives to the European Parliament, and at that time, before the introduction of direct elections, they were MPs drawn from both Houses. I was one of those approached to see if I would be interested in going to Strasbourg, and I indicated acceptance on the basis that I would oppose any extension of European political power or a political union. Strangely, I was not selected.

The 1970 Parliament saw the introduction of the Expenditure Select Committee, with several sub-committees, all of which have since become select committees in their own right. I took my place on the Environment Committee and soon afterwards was elected its chairman. Among our several studies was a massive report on transport, and I recall the awkward moment when Professor Peter Hall came to give his evidence, but there were only two MPs present. The quorum for the committee was three, but Hall was acknowledged as one of the greatest experts in the country, so I decided to forget the quorum rule and we took evidence for two hours, thereby greatly enhancing the value of our findings.

Our committee visited Munich, then widely considered the most advanced city in Europe from a transport perspective, with the added bonus of being taken to *The Flying Dutchman*. This proved to be a memorable performance, with just a triangle of sail appearing on the horizon, which grew bigger as it seemingly approached, until the full ship appeared and filled half the stage. It was quite the best production of the *Dutchman* that I have ever attended. The committee saw all that we needed to of the Bavarian solutions to road congestion. Rather than return with the other members at the end of the week, I went on to Vienna for a weekend of opera.

In previous Parliaments I had been too busy to go on Parliamentary visits abroad, but now I had time and thoroughly enjoyed some of the tours we went on which, at that time, were hardly jaunts to the fleshpots. My first visit was to Ethiopia, a nation in considerable economic difficulty and a recipient of well-intentioned aid from many different countries, although the results were somewhat mixed. We visited the sugar plantations and factory, run by the Dutch, which was supplying the whole country and selling as much as they could overseas. While this assisted the local economy by creating exports, there was unfortunately more than enough of a surplus to make sweets, which were ruining the teeth of the children. We also visited the American-sponsored agricultural college, where local farmers were taught to use fertilisers, which they could never hope to afford.

After these visits the members of the group split up, and as there was a war being waged against Somalia, I headed towards it to learn at first hand what was really happening. I reached the army headquarters, where I found the Indians were doing their bit by training the troops. In overall command was an Indian major-general whom I had known years earlier in India when I had been a major and he a subaltern. He was equally delighted to see me, but would not let me go to the front. I did, however, receive a detailed briefing on the local conflict, and returned to Addis Ababa better informed.

En route, I made a detour to a British team engaged in the campaign to eradicate locusts. Their work was potentially extremely valuable because of the annual infestation of these insects, which plagued the region. The team's activities had, however, been curtailed when one of their aircraft, used to spray the breeding groups, was shot down by the Ethiopian Air Force. I was advised that secret negotiations were under way to find a means of compensating the aid agency without any admission of Ethiopian liability; the delicacy of the situation required considerable discretion. Our group was therefore caused much embarrassment when one of our number, Julian Critchley, promptly sold the story to *The Times*, thereby wrecking the private talks.

I was irritated that a confidence had been compromised, and that one of our members should have been taking advantage of his Parliamentary position to enhance his journalism. This sort of incident was rare in those days, and taken seriously by the House authorities and the whips, but such views later came to be considered anachronistic. Then the abuses became endemic, and a committee was required to assess and impose standards in public life.

As our visit came to a conclusion, with Critchley suitably chastened, we were granted an audience with the Emperor. As the limousine swept us through Addis Ababa's broad avenues, all but devoid of traffic, our Ambassador briefed us. The Emperor was to be addressed by his full title of 'His Imperial Majesty, Emperor Haile Selassie I, King of Kings and Lord of Lords, Conquering Lion of the Tribe of Judah, Elect of God'. Aeroplanes were not to be mentioned. The palace had a dusty, slightly run-down air, with soldiers lounging at each gate. Within, it was dark and sparsely furnished in a style that would have looked dated at the time of Evelyn Waugh's visit in 1931. We were shown to the throne room and kept waiting the forty minutes predicted by the Ambassador. Eventually a small man in a white tunic, broad-faced and grizzled of beard, emerged from behind a curtain flanked by two palace guards with drawn swords; above this portal hung a very large and regal portrait of himself in full regalia.

To convey his displeasure over the aviation embarrassment the Lion of Judah declined to speak English, but nevertheless corrected his interpreter if any mistake was made in the translation from Amharic. The atmosphere thawed somewhat when I told him he was still warmly remembered in Bath. This was true, for after spending five years in exile there during the Italian occupation of 1936–41, he had donated his residence, Fairfield House, to the city as a home for the aged, which it remained.

By the time of our visit Haile Selassie was the longest-serving head of state and enjoyed considerable prestige, though he retained a sense of humour about himself – at least when among his peers. Attending the Shah of Iran's celebrations of 2,500 years since the founding of the Persian Empire at Isfahan in 1971, the monarchs present were transported to Persepolis by motor coach purportedly for security reasons; the Emperor, probably one of the few to have travelled by bus, passed down the vehicle exclaiming, 'Fares, please.'

Selassie was none the less somewhat embarrassed, as a devout Ethiopian Orthodox Christian, to be hailed as the living God by the Jamaican Rastafari sect, whose worship included the smoking of marijuana after blessing the pipes in the name of the 'Divine Selassie'. Despite a satisfactory state visit to Jamaica in 1966 the Emperor was at pains to discourage Rastafarian immigration. Nevertheless, when my son Julian visited Ethiopia in 2005 he found a small but thriving Rastafarian community puffing away at their sacrament to the tolerant puzzlement of their neighbours. They had been considerably irritated by the reinterment of Haile Selassie's body in the Cathedral of the Holy Trinity – 'He no dead, man. He immortal.'

Soon afterwards I went on another overseas visit, this time to Iran, a much more relaxed trip with plentiful caviar to ease its rigours. The itinerary included a visit to Isfahan. The Iranian senator who was to accompany us there was looking forward to bringing his mistress along too, but she got on too well with the actor MP Andrew Faulds on the first night in Tehran, so the senator left her behind. Undeterred, Faulds continued his hell-raising until it brought on a stroke and he was admitted to Tehran Hospital where the Empress was a patient. Soon he was to be seen flirting with her.

Apart from this rather undiplomatic episode, the rest of the visit went well, the way smoothed by the Foreign Minister. Ardeshir Zahedi was an old friend from his time as Iranian Ambassador to London, when he had routinely dispatched tins of caviar in place of 'thank-you' letters.

He arranged our audience with the Shah, who proved to be an imposing cold-eyed figure immaculately attired in a pinstripe Savile Row suit; this was in sober contrast to the Persian fancy dress of the palace guard. I asked why he permitted opium to be grown. The Shah looked at me closely, clearly unused to such impertinence. Clearing his throat, he explained that otherwise it would be smuggled in from

Afghanistan at a heavy cost in foreign currency. At the time this seemed an almost adequate explanation, for none of us could have anticipated the drug epidemic that would sweep the world.

A man of considerable presence enhanced by all the theatre of oriental panoply, Mohammad Reza Pahlavi, seemed utterly convincing; indeed such was his self-belief that he appeared to have persuaded himself – and Western governments – of the wisdom of his autocratic rule. Beneath Iran's calm surface dangerous tensions were brewing, however. That our diplomatic and intelligence services, although alarmed by the methods of SAVAK, his repressive secret police, should have so underestimated their extent remains puzzling given their involvement in his accession and subsequent close relations. There was certainly no hint of it on our Foreign Office briefing. The episode served to alert me to the limitations of intelligence, political and military, upon which I had relied in the field of war, particularly where it involved understanding a very different culture. The complexity of the Iranian situation and the strength of Islamic fervour had proved beyond our existing monitoring arrangements to interpret – and would so continue for the next quarter of a century.

The Anglo-Italian Parliamentary Group had been invited to send a party to Venice, and I was glad to be included in it. A high point of the visit was the loan of the chief of police's opera box at La Fenice for a performance of *Ballo in Maskera*. I explained to colleagues how the plot culminates in the murder of the King of Sweden. What I did not explain was that the opening production had been in Naples, where the royal censor did not take kindly to stories of royal assassination. It might have given the audience ideas about the unpopular Bourbon King Bomba. So for the Neapolitan production the story had been changed to the killing of the British Governor of Boston. Beyond Naples and the Kingdom of the Two Sicilies the Swedish version was the one used. When the curtain went up on the Boston version I was totally discredited.

On a Parliamentary visit to Canada, we flew direct to Saskatchewan, arriving about midnight our time, but in broad daylight to be invited to drinks and then dinner. My colleagues were all for bed but I rallied them with calls for another all-night sitting, lest we disappoint our hosts. The province faced a problem. It was their turn to host the Canadian Winter Games. There would be no shortage of snow, but the province

Meeting the Shah of Iran 1971. He offered an improbable explanation for opium growing.

Cheyne Walk, Chelsea. No 15 (second from right) was to become the family home for half a century.

Motor racing against the House of Lords, several of whose members had raced professionally, but were none the less dangerous for that.

Division Belle: An unfortunate incident at Cowes with James at the helm led to the Daring being dubbed *Collision Belle.*

is as flat as a waffle. It would not, however, have been done to cross the border to use the not far distant Rockies. The solution arrived at was to construct an artificial mountain.

In Ottawa I visited the National Gallery of Canada and that evening met its director. I told him that if he ever got tired of their Cranach, I would be glad to give it a home. He replied that Hermann Göring had felt the same way, and when the Germans invaded Holland, an officer had gone specially to relieve its Dutch owner of the picture. The gallery had purchased it after the war.

The Conservative Arts Committee, of which I was vice-chairman under Robert Cook, was invited to the National Gallery, London where we were shown the conservation department. The gallery wanted to clean Titian's 'Bacchus and Ariadne', its colour muted by brown varnish as the public had come to expect old masters to look. There would be an outcry when Titian's brilliant hues were exposed. So Robert and I wrote an encouraging letter to *The Times*, which the gallery could use as an alibi for the cleaning.

It is remarkable that of Titian's five great 'Poesies' painted for Charles V, three are now in Britain. When 'The Death of Actaeon' was due to be bought by the nation after agitation from the National Gallery, in order to tease them, I suggested in a letter to *The Times* that it should go to the Scottish National Gallery, to join 'Diana Surprised by Actaeon'. The ploy succeeded. The director immediately wrote condemning the Scottish Gallery as quite unsuited to care for such a precious picture, a suggestion that caused considerable offence in Edinburgh and an enjoyable row.

Visiting Paul Getty at Sutton Place, his sixteenth century Tudor estate in Surrey, he offered to show me his Raphael. To do so he unlocked his bedroom door, using three keys, and there was the Raphael beside his bed. I commented that at the Escorial Palace Philip II had a prized Titian opposite his bed so that he could gaze at it constantly, but Getty preferred the occasional look. Having founded the Getty Oil Company he had become the first dollar billionaire, although he later remarked that 'A billion isn't worth what it used to be'. Many of his assets – though not the Raphael – went into the collection of the J. Paul Getty Museum in California. While not quite the morose figure of folklore, Paul could hardly have been described as light-hearted, though he did have a dark sense of humour, implicit in the title of his first book, *How To Be Rich*. In his will he left a million free of tax to each of his mistresses – provided they were not married. So my friend Patrick de Laszlo lost his wife in order that she might qualify.

I was able to continue my interest in sailing, because in those years the House of Commons Yacht Club (HCYC) was quite active and occasionally was invited to send a team abroad to compete against other clubs with whom we had some connection. These were all-party events and served to develop friendships across party lines. The Labour members John Cronin and Reggie Paget, for example, were both keen yachtsmen and participated in our races, which rarely conflicted with the Parliamentary timetable. We had arranged a race against the Gibraltar Yacht Club at Easter 1970, but the General Election was called for May, so several members cried off. Nevertheless, Reggie Paget, Reggie Bennett and I went ahead and we received a warm welcome. The trip was especially memorable because Reggie Bennett found a place name, 'Wilson's Ramp', there and had himself photographed beside it.

A resident of one of Bembridge Harbour's famously scruffy and uncomfortable houseboats, Reggie was an ebullient character who was appointed the Queen's Yacht-Master upon the retirement of Uffa Fox. He was a frequent winner of the Imperial Poona Yacht Club's annual sailing-backwards race.

Until his death in the 1970s, the hospitable Monsieur André, Deauville's permanent mayor, used to invite teams from the British and French Parliaments and their families, for an annual weekend of sport. The golf and tennis teams competed against French MPs, the sailing team against the Deauville Yacht Club in their Dragons. We had to find our own way there, but Reggie Bennett, ever frugal, always thumbed a lift on Lord Verulam's plane.

One Saturday there was a freak storm on the Normandy coast, sinking a hundred yachts and blowing the roofs off houses, but we raced nevertheless. Reggie Paget tacked but the jib sheet jammed and a capsize was threatened. Reggie quickly produced a knife and cut the sheet, and even remembered to pay for the damage. The course called for a gybe at the weather mark but I sailed on and then tacked, gently easing the boat on to the downwind leg, rather than risk a broken mast. We were expecting a 'Shorten Course' flag, but as Reggie Bennett and I were first and second, we were sent round again in case the French could catch up. They didn't.

Once, at Deauville, there was a swimming race against the French MPs, but I tactlessly won by so much that the photographers lined the competitors up ten yards from the finish to get a better photograph. The race was not repeated. We always tried to make some return to Mayor André by visiting his casino.

At Whitsun 1971 we were invited to take a team to Bermuda to helm five Solings against the Royal Bermuda Yacht Club. To make up our numbers we had to call upon the House of Lords Yacht Club, so we took out three MPs and three peers. Unfortunately Lord Rankeiller turned out not to be much of a sailor, having merely come for the ride, so there was no relief for the other five of us. Since our opponents were the Olympic team, we were beaten quite thoroughly, but Sir Freddie Bennett, who owned an inland island near St George's, flew from Canada to give a drinks party and commiserate with us. Freddie was a Commons character and had often mentioned his home in Bermuda, one of several he owned, including an Elizabethan castle at Kingswear, overlooking the Dart estuary in Devon, and a large estate in Wales. Naturally, our expectations were high, but we soon discovered that, unlike many islands in Bermuda, which are beautifully kept, Freddie's was tiny, in the middle of a swamp and covered in scrub. His tropical home turned out to be not much more than a two-roomed hut, apparently devoid of any cooking or other facilities, so we drank standing up in a small clearing. The whole Bermuda Cabinet was there, but not the Governor or our peers, who perhaps had been warned of what to expect.

Despite this defeat, the HCYC became increasingly popular and when, the following year, I was elected Commodore, five of us subscribed to build a Daring to race in that class at Cowes. *Division Belle* proved a huge success, allowing members of the syndicate to participate in the challenging one-design competitions throughout the summer, and compete in the annual Cowes Week regatta. John Hannam, Micky Grylls, John Cronin and I regularly took the helm, and the only MP not to do so was Edward du Cann, who generously subscribed to *Division Belle*'s purchase price, but then never sailed in her. The Parliamentary influence over the class was enhanced by Boz Ferranti (later to acquire the rather grand title of Vice-President of Europe), who owned *Ding Dong*, and his wife Hillary who shared *Finesse*.

Although our leader, Ted Heath, appeared to many as rather austere, a solitary unapproachable figure mainly interested in music, he was an enthusiastic yachtsman and enjoyed Cowes. These were not, however, interests that made him popular, and his government was in terminal decline, with such miscalculations as the belief that High Court judges could sensibly intervene in industrial disputes, or that the coal miners could not hold the country to ransom. A clever young lawyer, Geoffrey Howe, had in Opposition produced a draft law that would infallibly deal with trade union abuses; when applied by the Heath government it failed miserably.

My own constituency, losing the electorally attractive town of Harpenden in a boundary adjustment, was threatened, leaving me very vulnerable in the modern estates of Hemel Hempstead. Many of the inhabitants had been rehoused by the New Towns Commission from the East End: they were not natural Conservatives.

Among my constituents, Paul Boateng was the son of Ghana's Attorney-General; he later told me he had attended all of my campaign meetings to confirm his commitment to the Labour Party. He subsequently became the first black Cabinet minister, serving in the Blair government before being appointed British High Commissioner to South Africa over the heads of senior diplomats.

Another constituent was Graham Young, the notorious poisoner. In one of his many letters from prison protesting his innocence, and insisting that the death of most of his family had been a tragic accident unconnected with his interest in lethal toxins, he had begged me to press the Home Office for his immediate release – and to get him a job with Kodak, the largest local employer. Having taken advice, I learned that Young had become the world's leading expert on the deadly effects of thallium, and work in a chemical laboratory of the kind used by Kodak to process photographic film would almost certainly amount to a death sentence for the rest of the workforce.

15

Leaving Parliament

Heath wanted to call an election in January 1974 when the issue of the miners' strike was paramount. But the Party Chairman, Lord Carrington, who never quite lived up to his reputation for competence, was not ready with the manifesto. When the General Election was called in February 1974, the Labour and Liberal manifestos were on the bookstalls, while I had to make do with a single typed copy of the Tory manifesto for the entire constituency.

During the ensuing election, Keith Joseph came to speak for me at Berkhamsted. This strange, gloomy but brilliant man, nicknamed 'the mad monk', was promoting the use of market forces, later to be known as 'Thatcherism'. I invited him to a meal beforehand, but he preferred an hour of silent contemplation in a lay-by with a glass of milk. The packed audience was eager to hear the sage's wise views on current events, but instead Keith spoke of the evils of single-parent families. Why had he chosen to speak on a subject of no great interest in wealthy Berkhamsted, where I knew of no current cases? No explanation was forthcoming. Indeed the only single-parent family anyone could recall in Berkhamsted had consisted of Lady Blanche Hozier, who had lived in a small house in the High Street, with her daughter Clementine, later to marry Winston Churchill.

After the meeting, I told Keith that not all single-parent families contained feckless unmarried mothers: there were also widows and widowers, husbands abandoned by their wives and wives whose partners had disappeared. Nevertheless Keith repeated the speech later in the year in Lancashire, attracting great hostile publicity. This apparent heartlessness halted his political career, and he found himself lacking the support to challenge Ted Heath for the leadership. Thus Keith's lesser-known disciple, Margaret Thatcher, took his place, which was probably just as well. Had Keith been Prime Minister, I doubt that he would have had the imprudence to send a fleet into hostile waters to rescue a tiny bit of the unfashionable British Empire. So because Keith ignored my criticism the Falkland Islanders are free!

At the General Election my majority dropped from 11,000 to 400, while in the Commons there was a near dead heat, which allowed Harold Wilson to form a minority government when Heath's efforts to do so failed. Of course, this arrangement could not last long, and we all realised that another General Election must come soon.

Margaret Thatcher was appointed Shadow Environment Minister and Chairman of the Conservative Environment Committee, and I was elected her vice-chairman, but there was little time for discussions on future policy because the next manifesto was needed quickly. Margaret, whose powers of memory were exceptional, wrote into it the promise to extend the sale of council houses to flats. I informed her that I had spent the last four years trying to persuade the department to do just that, but it had insisted the proposal was quite impracticable. Margaret asked, 'Do you want me to take it out?' Naturally enough my answer was, 'Leave it in.'

Just as the October 1974 election was announced, the Conservative committee of one of my best towns collapsed, but my son Rupert, aged twenty-two and full of political ambition, volunteered to work full-time during the election, and I assigned the task of canvassing the town to him. After ten days he announced the electoral roll 90 per cent canvassed, a new committee at work and a Young Conservative branch formed. I then sent him to repeat the process in another branch, where the elderly committee seemed to be doing nothing. He was able to report a 100 per cent canvass by polling day, and this was nearly enough to win despite the unfavourable circumstances prevailing in the country. In the event the constituency was lost by two hundred votes, and Harold Wilson obtained a working majority.

I left the Commons with mixed feelings: history had been made during my time there, and I had had the opportunity of coming to know most of the principal players on the political stage. Yet I had a sense that there were great changes in store, but that they would require steadiness of purpose to overcome entrenched interests, notably the opposition of the trades unions to reform of our archaic labour laws.

My consolation was that Rupert was soon adopted as the prospective Parliamentary candidate for Kettering, where my old schoolfriend from

Haileybury, Geoffrey de Freitas, was the Labour member. Rupert soon established himself as an outstandingly good candidate. In these circumstances I felt I could retire, but would remain active in politics through my membership of the association. In the early 1970s Bill Deedes had asked me to take his place as the Conservative representative on the executive committee of the influential Town and Country Planning Association (TCPA), a body with distinctly left-wing leanings. I was to stay aboard for almost ten years, becoming its nominee on the Environment Council's Transport Committee. Eventually I resigned from the TCPA in protest at its vehement opposition to nuclear energy. I believed our policy should favour a cheap and abundant source of energy that would not poison the atmosphere. It was sad that a hitherto respectable environmental body should join the anti-nuclear lobby out of misplaced dogma. The consequence of its success has been that Britain now buys power from France, generated by nuclear power in Normandy, where the prevailing wind would carry any emissions not over France, but to the south coast of England. But alarm seems misplaced. As an American friend pointed out, in the USA more people have died in the back seat of Teddy Kennedy's car than from nuclear emission.

The Environment Council had been set up on the initiative of the Duke of Edinburgh to provide government with concerted advice on environmental matters, rather than the confusion of conflicting views from single-interest pressure groups. I had soon been elected chairman of the Transport Committee, and for the next fifteen years ensured that the Ministry of Transport understood our views. During the Thatcher government I knew all the ministers personally, so if I asked for an interview, I got it, and when a minister came to speak at one of our conferences, he did not just make his speech and depart, as is customary, but stayed to the end and listened. Recognition came when the government decreed that environmental issues should always be considered in forming policy, a notion considered radical at the time.

During the Heath government, the Buchanan Report on the siting of the third London airport was published. There was little consideration of environmental matters and the first choice was Cublington, a village in open countryside in Bedfordshire. It was just over the border from my constituency, where we had plenty of experience of the nuisance created by low-flying aircraft, since we lay on the flight path from Luton Airport. I was deeply anxious, but I need not have worried, for Lady Pamela Berry, wife of the proprietor of the *Daily Telegraph*, had a country house at Cublington and she put her tiny foot down. In those days three families controlled most of the English newspapers and if their interests were threatened they united. So the press carried thunderous denunciations of the choice of Cublington and the government switched to the second alternative, Foulness, but changed its name to Maplin because that sounded better.

Freed from the restrictions of three-line whips, back-bench committee meetings and constituency engagements, I was able to continue some of my sports. I had long given up hunting and polo, but I had continued to shoot, ski and sail, and had been delighted when entering the Commons to find that these very sports were popular with my Parliamentary colleagues.

Soon after I had entered the Commons I had been recruited to participate in the Anglo-Swiss Parliamentary ski-race at Davos in January 1960. In those days Swiss MPs had not been particularly agile, and we were able to hold our own in the giant slalom competition. In later years however, when national honour was at stake, the Swiss began to elect ski teachers and even former Olympic skiers. Despite this we obtained surprisingly good results, winning in 1960, and had looked set to win again the following year. Our captain, Ernest Marples, made us take an early run down the course shortly before nine o'clock, when it was solid ice. I fell awkwardly and broke my ankle, so we just lost the race, much to the relief of the Swiss team.

Undeterred by this initiation, I continued to participate in the annual event for many years, as the rules were relaxed to allow ex-members to participate. I was to witness my sons and grandsons compete in the followers' race, thereby making the annual trip to Davos a real family, as well as a Parliamentary, event. Warm friendships were developed with our Swiss counterparts, including the ever-generous René Bühler, and whenever the opportunity arose we reciprocated with hospitality in London.

Some of the members of the Lords and Commons became regular attendees at Davos, and my friends Jack Diamond, Bryant Godman-Irvine and Philip Goodhart joined me as veteran participants. Among the best skiers on our team were Winston Churchill, Michael Ancram and Charlie Lyell, while Toby Jessell ensured that the bloodwagon and

JHA continued competing in the Anglo-Swiss MP race until his 80th year when he won the veteran's cup.

Historic Cabinet 21st June 1979

Left to right (standing): Norman Fowler, Transport Minister; John Biffen, Chief Secretary to the Treasury; David Howell, Energy Secretary; Norman St John Stevas, Chancellor of the Duchy of Lancaster; Humphrey Atkins, Northern Ireland Secretary; George Younger, Scottish Secretary; Michael Heseltine, Environment Secretary; Nicholas Edwards, Welsh Secretary; Patrick Jenkin, Social Services Secretary; John Nott, Trade Secretary; Mark Carlisle, Education Secretary; Angus Maude, Paymaster General; and Sir John Hunt, Secretary to the Cabinet.

Left to right (seated): Sir Ian Gilmour, Lord Privy Seal; Lord Soames, Lord President of the Council; Sir Keith Joseph, Industry Secretary; Lord Carrington, Foreign Secretary; William Whitelaw, Home Secretary; Margaret Thatcher, Prime Minister; Lord Hailsham, Lord Chancellor; Sir Geoffrey Howe, Chancellor of the Exchequer; Francis Pym, Defence Minister; James Prior, Employment Secretary; and Peter Walker, Agriculture Minister.

Photo by Keystone/Getty Images

the town's famous *krankenhaus* had plenty of work. Although for many years the team was dominated by Tories, we did acquire Social Democrats, Paddy Ashdown and John Wilkinson, and a cross-bencher or two, such as James Norton. One consequence of the Blair era was that New Labour ceased regarding the sport as elitist, and Dennis MacShane was able to show off his language skills, eventually succeeding John Hannam as our captain.

One year the Rank Organisation invited the Parliamentary ski team to compete against theirs at Aviemore in the Highlands, where they were opening a hotel. Rank directors constantly eat large meals, and most weighed about twenty stone, but we found that they had recruited extremely athletic juniors. On the Saturday, the wind was too high to permit any skiing, but we were woken on Sunday morning with the news that the wind had now dropped to forty knots. On the nursery slopes, all snow had been blown away, but many lads and lassies were there learning to ski. An American commented to me, 'I thought the British were effete, but now I know they are the master race.' On the Monday, there was a blue cloudless sky and no wind, so we raced the slalom on sheet ice, and lost.

As well as skiing in the Parliamentary team, over the years I represented the Commons at bridge in matches against the House of Lords, motor racing at Brands Hatch, shooting, and swimming.

16

Travels

While I was still in the Commons I had made it a policy not to travel behind the Iron Curtain.

Soon after leaving Parliament, however, I made a week's tour to Moscow and St Petersburg and, returning to my room in Moscow unexpectedly during the day, found the floorboards up and an electrician scrutinising a mass of wires. He was presumably checking my microphone, which had recorded absolutely nothing. Our Intourist guide arranged a visit to the circus, but when I said I preferred the Bolshoi, she said this was impossible because their star ballerina was appearing in *Giselle*. Undeterred by her advice, I walked up and down outside the Bolshoi, but the first three who approached me wanted to buy tickets. The fourth had one for sale, but preferred cigarettes to roubles. I offered a box of chocolates, which was eagerly accepted. This was the kind of petty black-market activity, endemic in Moscow, that was routinely used to entrap foreigners, but I was no longer a target for anyone.

My next visit behind the Iron Curtain was to Prague on an opera tour organised by a British company. They relied upon a local man to buy the opera tickets, but he had been ill and failed them, so the many old ladies on the tour had to miss their opera. Knowing, however, how the system worked in the Eastern bloc, I bribed the chief attendant, and got into every opera. My next visit to St Petersburg was on an arts tour organised as the first of a series by a young man who commissioned several experts each of whom taught the others so that on later tours a single expert could give all the talks. One afternoon we were due for a talk in the Hermitage's Rembrandt room, but when we got there it was closed for redecoration. A message was sent that a great English expert on Rembrandt was present, but there followed a long wait during which many of the group drifted away; but at last we were allowed in and given a talk on the twenty paintings.

That evening a friend in the party expressed her disappointment at having missed it, and said she would go the following morning. I assured here that she could not gain entrance, but she insisted she could get in anywhere. The next morning I pointed out the locked door, but then along came a janitor with a bunch of keys, followed by a European couple. My friend recognised her ex-son-in-law, so we all went in and I gave them the lecture I had heard the day before. The tour was a success and the advance bookings for future tours were so good that the young man, Sir Rupert Mackeson, absconded to Rhodesia with the deposits.

For my next visit to St Petersburg, I went on a package tour. On the day we were to have a guided tour of the Hermitage, I left the party on entry at 9.30 a.m. and went straight to the Leonardo room. There I had ten minutes alone with the two beautiful small Madonnas before the first of the guided tours arrived, which would engulf the Leonardos for the rest of the day.

I had a similar experience with Vermeer. At The Hague a special exhibition of thirty-five paintings was crammed into the downstairs rooms of the Mauritshuis. The result was crowds seven deep before each painting. So when the London National Gallery mounted a smaller Vermeer exhibition, I took the precaution of going to a private evening view for members of the National Art Collection Fund. There the crowds were only four deep, until a Vermeer lecture was announced and everyone departed to attend. So I was left for half an hour alone with an entire Vermeer collection.

In the 1980s I visited Warsaw, where memories of the 1944 uprising were still fresh. The Red Army had been rapidly approaching the city, and when it was only fifteen miles away the resistance movement rose up against the Germans. Stalin halted the Russian forces while his two enemies destroyed each other. Britain wished to drop arms and supplies to the Poles, but the distance was such that the aircraft needed to refuel behind the Russian lines; permission was refused.

The uprising was eventually suppressed with the loss of a quarter of a million Polish lives. Hitler ordered the city centre to be utterly destroyed. It became the only city where you could stand in its centre and watch the sun rise and set. The Poles had since re-created the market square, using as reference the paintings of Bellotto, the nephew of Canaletto. Happily, Bellotto was very exact and detailed in his draughtsmanship, unlike Canaletto who indulged in artistic licence. They were even able to reproduce the exact mouldings on cornices. The paintings now hang in the rebuilt Royal Castle.

I kept quiet about my Polish link. In the 1920s my cousin Joyous Markham had married Count Wychinski. At the outbreak of the Second World War he was Polish Ambassador in London, and at the time of my visit he remained the senior member of the Polish government in exile. We saw his Warsaw palace taken over as the city library. Sadly, he did not live to see his country freed.

Another exile was Count Zamoyski, who was passionate about horse breeding. Although vehemently anti-communist, as a patriot he had, at the end of the war, traced, collected and restored to his country the Polish National Stud. He wrote a book about British bloodstock breeding, later telling me that the only person expert enough to criticise it was the Queen.

Another good friend was Baron Robert Vaess, Belgian Ambassador in London in the 1980s. Before that, in Brussels, he had been in bed with the wife of the German Ambassador when her husband arrived home unexpectedly. Robert had to hide in a cupboard. The German opened the cupboard and said, 'Wass ist das?' The inevitable reply was, 'Das ist Vaess.'

At this time one of the leading figures in café society was Charles Clore, the property developer, a man fawned upon by every headwaiter in the West End on account of his lavish entertaining. He was to meet his Waterloo, however. Having built the Hilton Hotel in Park Lane he decided to throw a dinner party at his house in Park Street, to be followed by nightcaps in the top-floor restaurant of the Hilton. He and I arrived there first, and he inquired of the headwaiter whether his table was ready, expecting the reply, 'But, of course, Mr Clore, sir, the best table by the window.' But, instead, the conversation ran as follows. 'I don't know, sir – have you booked?' 'Yes, of course, I have booked.' 'In what name, sir?' 'Clore.' 'And how do you spell that?'

After glasnost, I spotted an advance notice that Tchaikovsky's opera *Mazeppa* was to be performed in St Petersburg. I very much wanted to see a good performance, as the Coliseum production in modern dress had been dreadful, so I booked for a weekend there. Then my daughter-in-law, Nicole, told me she was going out the same weekend, as my son, Rupert, a military historian specialising in espionage, had arranged to meet a retired KGB officer. In order to be with them I upgraded my hotel, at the cost of £200 a night, so it proved to be one of the most expensive telephone calls I have ever made. In St Petersburg our new KGB friend showed us the room Lenin had occupied in 1917, with his camp bed, desk and telephone, a rare sight unavailable to tourists as it is within City Hall.

Leaving the Commons also allowed me more time for bridge, but although I had played several times at the Portland Club, I had never joined as I had always considered the standard – and the stakes – a little too high for me. At that time the Portland's chairman was Selim Zilkha, the owner of Mothercare, whose Lebanese wife had recently run off with Harold Lever, Harold Wilson's Chief Secretary to the Treasury, and an equally wealthy man. Lever was an agreeable fellow, except at the bridge table where, after every hand, he insisted on describing each mistake that had been made. As he could hardly appear at the Portland, he played at the St James's Bridge Club until the other members could bear him no longer. Coincidentally, Zilkha chose this moment to sell Mothercare and move to New York, thus allowing Lever to join the Portland. I was entertained on one occasion when Margaret Thatcher, facing Lever across the despatch box during a financial debate, declared, 'There are five ways of making money. You can inherit it; you can marry it; you can win it by gambling or by speculation; and you can even earn it. The Right Honourable Gentleman has done all five!'

The ballet and the opera were passions I could indulge in my retirement, and I attended many magnificent performances. Among the most memorable was a sumptuous production at the Palais Garnier in Paris of *Robert le Diable* by Meyerbeer. The performance lasted five hours, with wonderful scenery and a huge cast in sumptuous costumes. In an effort to economise, the production had opted for unknowns instead of established stars, and the then unknown young singers from the United States included June Anderson, Chris Merrett and Samuel Ramey, all to become great international stars.

Another consuming interest has been art galleries, particularly those that reflect the taste of a single collector. Thus I have been an occasional visitor at the Frick in New York, the Isabella Stewart Gardner in Boston, the Wallace Collection in London, the Mauritshuis at The

Hague, the Ca D'Oro in Venice and the Borghese in Rome. I exclude the Thyssen in Madrid, which comprises a single example of almost every important old master, in my opinion a manifestation of mere Teutonic thoroughness. Frustratingly, when public buildings close for repairs in Italy they close their doors for up to fifteen years, and this happened at both the Ca D'Oro and the Borghese. When eventually the Borghese reopened the entry tickets were sold out three days in advance, and my pleas to make a visit were rejected.

On a visit to Berlin, my son Rupert asked me to photograph the wireless masts at a historic Allied signals intercept station that throughout the Cold War had eavesdropped on Eastern bloc communications. The site, known as Teufelsberg, had been constructed in 1946 from all the bomb rubble in Berlin. Formerly the location of the Luftwaffe's officers' academy, the area around it had been flattened by Allied air-raids; the site had then been designated to receive all the debris, thereby creating a man-made mountain. As the only significant hill between Berlin and the Czech and Polish borders, the Allies had taken advantage of its height to construct antennae on the summit, giving command of Warsaw Pact radio traffic across the horizon.

I climbed the mountain until I reached the barbed wire marking the perimeter, and started taking photographs. Suddenly a helicopter took off and flew towards me, prompting alarmed memories of *North by North-West* in which Cary Grant is pursued by a hostile aircraft. Despite this I managed to complete my assignment with only limited damage to my trousers. It was all for nothing: Whitehall had what was described as a 'conniption' and threatened prosecution should the photographs be published in the book intended, *GCHQ: The Secret Wireless War*.

On my next visit I flew to East Berlin to take a train to Leipzig but found the railway station in chaos. Checkpoint Charlie had been opened that very day to allow East Germans to visit West Berlin, where they were presented with fifty Deutschmarks each to spend. Not surprisingly, all trains were crowded with happy East Germans loaded with electrical appliances. That weekend I watched the historic sight of anti-communist marches in Leipzig and East Berlin, the very first not suppressed by Erich Honecker's crumbling regime.

This was but one of many visits to Germany, and on one occasion I attended a performance at the Wiesbaden opera house. This little gem, built in the nineteenth century, had been a favourite of the Kaiser. I learned that the city had been spared any Allied bombing during the Second World War because it had been selected as the US Air Force's post-war headquarters. I mused that the fortunate inhabitants must have wondered what ghastly fate was in store for them when everywhere else in Germany had been devastated.

Besides my visits abroad, I used to travel for weekends all over England to visit performances of regional opera companies. Scottish Opera came as far south as Newcastle. One year, Welsh National Opera toured a superb production of *Parsifal*, directed and conducted by Reginald Goodall. It quickly sold out at every venue except Liverpool, whence some genius placed advertisements in London to 'join the Parsifal Express'. So at 2 p.m. on a Saturday I caught the express at Euston. The performance was interrupted by a long interval, during which supper was laid on at the Adelphi Hotel as part of the package. We arrived back at Euston station at 4 a.m. in pouring rain. At last I got a taxi, and the driver said to me, 'You're out a bit late, ain't you, guv'nor?' I replied 'You won't believe this but I have been to Liverpool for the day.'

On a visit to the Edinburgh Festival, I called at the Edinburgh Museum and asked to see the sedan chair of my great-great-great grandfather, Professor James Hamilton, the pioneer of obstetrics. I was directed to an exhibition of the distinguished figures of the late eighteenth century who had comprised the Scottish Enlightenment, Adam Smith, David Hume, Robert Adam among them.

Standing beside his sedan chair was an effigy of the professor, with a small screen in place of a face, on to which was projected a talking film, so that he appeared to be speaking in a most convincing way. So thick with mud in winter were the streets of Edinburgh, he said, that the only way to get about was by chair: it was essential to ensure that your chair men were sober. I am probably the only man to have been spoken to by an ancestor six generations back.

In those days when members of Lloyd's still received a cheque every June, I used to buy paintings by minor old masters. To get them cleaned I went to a young Pole employed by several West End art dealers, who had been trained at the Courtauld Institute. He told me of a client who had bought an old master in Rome. In order to export it, he had a modern daub painted over it. My restorer duly removed the daub, but reported that there was an earlier painting underneath the 'old master'. This turned out to be the head of Benito Mussolini.

I bought a painting by David Teniers the younger of a pretty Dutch girl holding a bunch of flowers. The restorer was sure that something else was concealed, so I agreed to a cleaning. A fortnight later he telephoned me with the words, 'Do you remember my story of the head of Mussolini?' My heart sank, but it turned out to be the head of Holofernes, and the young girl was his nemesis, Judith. Not long afterwards in the Gemäldegalerie in Berlin I saw a Teniers painting, *The Artist and His Family*. His wife is quite clearly the model for Judith. She was the daughter of Jan ('Velvet') Bruegel. Marrying into the Breugel family, friends of Rubens, had done Teniers's career no harm. I subsequently found Mrs Teniers in many of his larger paintings, but never depicted as a peasant, always being painted in a fine dress. In the Metropolitan Museum, New York, there is a very similar picture of Judith – same mode-same dress-different pose – evidently painted at the same time as mine.

I did not usually buy 'school of' paintings, since I prefer an original to a copy. But when I saw a 'School of Watteau' painting on sale at Sotheby's from the Lowther Castle Collection I was struck by its absolute beauty. I could not find anything similar in Watteau's work, so I took it to the Wallace Collection, where the curator brought out the book of engravings of the hundred or so paintings of Nicholas Lancret. There was my painting, *Les Charmes de le Conversation*, original marked as lost. Mine indeed turned out to be the original. During the French Revolution the then Earl of Lonsdale was buying pictures brought over by French émigrés and my picture must have been mis-catalogued and disregarded. Wildenstein of New York are preparing a book of coloured illustrations of Lancret's paintings. It will include mine.

Such had been the success of Sir Robert Walpole as prime minister that he was able to build Houghton Hall in Norfolk and fill it with old masters. Here he was in competition with the rulers of several German states, who were building the magnificent collections at Berlin, Dresden, Munich and Kassel. But after the Seven Years War they could no longer afford to collect, so Catherine the Great had the field to herself. Alas Walpole's grandson was a spendthrift, and had to sell the collection of paintings. Catherine bought the lot and they helped to fill the Hermitage. After glasnost, the Hermitage lent the Walpole collection for exhibition in England, and it was displayed at Kenwood. Visiting, I was surprised to find that the custodian guarding the last room was the Marquess of Cholmondeley, the owner by inheritance of Houghton, and with whom I played bridge at White's. Having visited Houghton, and knowing that they had the catalogue showing where every painting had hung there, I suggested how romantic it would be if they could be returned there just for once. But he could envisage only the disturbance to his home.

My great-grandfather, Thomas Allason, was born in 1790 over his father's bookshop in Bond Street. He became a distinguished classical architect, and had eight children. But I was the only male Allason of my generation, so it fell to me to give him a bicentennial party. Over a hundred of his descendants met under his portrait by Lawrence in a room at Sotheby's, a few doors from his birthplace. They were presented with a family tree, made complicated by an Allason uncle and nephew marrying sisters, so many were double cousins, some meeting for the first time.

My last visit overseas was to New York, at the age of ninety and nearly blind. I used a wheelchair at the airports and stayed at a hotel close to the Metropolitan Opera. The purpose was to see Bellini's *Il Pirata*, which is staged very rarely. It was given magnificent treatment by the Met, including Renee Fleming at the height of her considerable vocal powers. I flew back on the day-flight to Heathrow, and, economical as ever, took the Underground to Sloane Square. Unknown to me, I was shadowed by an official to ensure that the poor old blind man got through. He introduced himself, however, and when he said that he had been on the Berlin Airlift, I was able to share my part in organising it from Whitehall.

For my seventieth birthday my sons had presented me with a pennant to replace that flown from my squadron commander's tank during the war. This raised some interesting heraldic questions. Cue the entry of a most splendid figure, Peter Drummond Murray of Mastrick, Slains Pursuivant of Arms to the Lord High Constable of Scotland, and highly esteemed at the Court of the Lord Lyon King of Arms in Edinburgh. A considerable wit, with an encyclopaedic knowledge of heraldry, and indeed of Scottish history, Slains cast a quizzical eye over the coat of arms long employed by the family. 'Allason, aye. But no' your branch o' the family,' he concluded with a shake of his tabard. 'But we'll soon remedy that.'

The Allasons, it emerged from researches conducted by Slains's scribes, were indeed a sept of MacDonald of Clanranald, and had quite properly worn that discreet tartan along with the more lurid Allason plaid. In no time Ranald MacDonald, Captain of Clanranald, chief of the name and arms of the clan, appeared at White's, checking his claymore with the porter, to append his name to a bond of manrent drawn up by Slains. To Julian's mild alarm this committed the senior Allason to depute one of his sons to lead a troop of horse in support of any adventures embarked upon by the Captain of Clanranald. Given the present office holder's colourful reputation, it did not seem impossible that he might declare war upon another clan, if not upon England.

Slains was consoling. As personal herald to the Earl of Erroll, hereditary Lord High Constable of Scotland and superior of the GOC Scottish forces, he felt confident of his ability to nip any such insurrection in the bud. Whether the General would obey an order from the Constable to incarcerate Clanranald in Edinburgh Castle has yet to be put to the test. Relations with the other MacDonald chiefs, however, remain sufficiently tense for the possibility not to be ruled out entirely.

After a meeting with Lyon and his glamorous blonde clerk a new achievement of new arms was approved, based upon, but appropriately differenced from, the Clanranald arms. Tactfully the lion crest long used on family silver was retained. Such were the complexity and fine detail of the new arms that the heraldic artist subsequently demanded a bonus. Slains became a family friend and counsellor, generously risking his reputation with an offer to put Julian's son Jamie up for the New Club in Edinburgh.

18

Conclusion

The first twenty years of my life were merely a preparation for what was to come. Then an astonishing change took place. One year, I was a harshly disciplined Gentleman Cadet, the next saw me hunting, skiing, playing polo and owning a Bentley. At 49p a day my pay might well have served to curtail these activities, but fortunately I had a modest private income, which was just enough to enable me to enjoy life for the next three-quarters of a century.

As a boy I was troubled by the biblical injunction to sell all one's goods, but it appeared to me pointless unless everybody did the same. I preferred the parable of the talents, which seems to approve of the accumulation of wealth. Although there is great poverty in the world, matters are relative. My Indian servants were very happy on £1 a month. During the Second World War, I fancied a flat with central heating and a self-change radiogram would be the height of luxury. No thought of television or foreign travel, now commonplace.

When I entered the House of Commons, the salary was £1,500 a year, out of which one had to pay a secretary. I spent more doing the job than I received, so that I felt a sense of independence rather than of being a paid public servant. Bob Mellish, Labour MP for Bermondsey, told me that he could not afford a secretary, so had to write all his constituency letters in long-hand. His brother, a police sergeant, was far better remunerated. The pendulum has now swung in the opposite direction.

I thoroughly enjoyed my four years as a back-seat driver at the War Office. The really hard work, however, came during the next six years in Opposition. One had to watch constantly for government attempts to pull dirty tricks on the public, to expose and fight them. A contemporary example would be the 'stealth taxes' concealed by

Gordon Brown in the small print of successive budget statements, and which the citizen comprehends only when they hit him. Such vigilance had its cost. Sometimes I found myself working ninety or a hundred hours a week – hardly conducive to family life.

One thing I swiftly learnt in government. If there is a problem, the civil service will counsel throwing money at it. But when you do so, the money goes on more civil servants, not on solving the problem. The natural desire of the mandarin is to expand his or her sphere of activity, employ more staff, and to receive promotion. Such momentum does this tendency enjoy that it requires a conscious effort to prevent government expanding. Since 1997 the public sector has again grown bloated – privatisation notwithstanding – to the extent that in Scotland and the north the private sector can no longer support it from tax revenues. This is a time bomb ticking away beneath the union.

During my service in the Commons the party was led by three prime ministers, Harold Macmillan, Alec Home and Ted Heath, and I endured two of Harold Wilson's premierships. All four were remarkable men, but each seemed to me to be slightly flawed.

'Supermac' was really a wonderful actor, a superb conviction politician who was quite right when he told the electorate 'You've never had it so good.' Most finance ministers would be delighted to have accomplished a fraction of what Derick Heathcote-Amory achieved as Chancellor of the Exchequer. One of Macmillan's handicaps was his pretence that he had sprung from humble crofting roots in the Highlands, whereas his grandfather, far from being impoverished, had been a prosperous bookseller in Edinburgh. One of my own forebears had owned a bookshop in Bond Street. More significantly, Harold was always burdened by the loss of so many of his contemporaries in France during the Great War, and on a personal level he was quite unapproachable on issues relating to the private lives of public figures. He, of course, had very personal reasons for being sensitive on this topic, but his isolation contributed to the Profumo tragedy.

Alec, however, had the misfortune to be an honest man in an era that demanded a telegenic presence, a quality even his most fervent admirers would claim he never possessed. He was exactly what he appeared to be, a blue-blooded Scottish landowner committed to public service. Nevertheless, he was lampooned for remaining true to his background. His fatal flaw, as far as I was concerned, was his ability to make those sitting behind him wince when he showed that his years in the Lords had put him so far out of touch with the electorate.

By contrast, Harold Wilson was a genius at disguising his background, political opinions and objectives. As a middle-aged Oxford don, fond of a cigar and a balloon of fine Cognac, he successfully persuaded the public that he was a youthful, pipe-smoking technocrat in touch with the aspirations of the Beatles generation. He was nothing of the kind, but he played the role with skill and, as we would now recognise, with considerable spin. Who can forget Wilson's disgraceful broadcast in which he insisted that devaluation would not affect the value of the pound? There is a line between political pragmatism and insulting dishonesty, and Wilson overstepped it on many occasions. As well as setting an appalling example, he allowed others to behave badly too, and one can only wonder at what kind of a hold some of those closest to him had over him. Nevertheless, only a political genius could manage a Cabinet containing the ambitious Jim Callaghan, the scheming Denis Healey, the shrewish Barbara Castle, a loony Tony Benn and a drunken George Brown.

In truth, Ted was the true technocrat. Both Wilson and Heath had been civil servants, and doubtless both should have remained in Whitehall and not opted for Westminster. Whereas Wilson had a talent for being all things to all people, Ted made absolutely no attempt to ingratiate himself with either the party or his Parliamentary colleagues. I put his boorish aloofness down to a crippling shyness, and I saw him really at ease only among his sailing companions.

In retrospect, I now realise that Ted's obsession with Europe, founded in his wartime experience in Normandy, had clouded his judgement to the point that he willingly deceived us when he glibly gave assurances that joining the Common Market would not compromise Britain's sovereignty. Now we know better, but during the referendum campaign qualified majority voting had not yet entered the lexicon. The paradox is that Ted's original 1970 election manifesto, based on policies agreed at the famous Selsdon Park gathering, amounted to a truly Conservative, market-driven formula for rescuing the country from Wilsonian socialism, yet Ted abandoned all those guiding principles when threatened by high unemployment, obsolescent industry and militant trade unions. Ted's U-turn is well documented, but he never could bring himself to admit he had reneged on almost every commitment he had made.

There were some excuses for Ted's failure. He could not compete with trade union power after the failure of Geoffrey Howe's industrial legislation. Ted's underlying instincts were corporatist: he once demanded of me, 'Are you saying that Britain cannot afford Maplin, Concorde and the Channel Tunnel at the same time – when each Canadian province has a project as big as these?' I wonder if he was telling the truth, for I never heard of any such projects when I visited Canada.

It was left to Margaret to pick up the pieces, and occasionally I regret I could not have cheered her on in the Commons as she championed council house sales, pioneered privatisation and restored Britain's image abroad. She possessed none of the flaws of her predecessors, and I was heartened by her swift promotion of Cecil Parkinson and Norman Tebbit. But what would have happened if she had won the Hemel Hempstead selection for 1959, and then lost her seat in October 1974?

My life was also mapped out in cars. The first was a Morris Minor, which would do 65 mph downhill with the wind behind it. For my 21st birthday I bought a ten-year-old three litre Bentley open four-seater and started to enjoy motor sport, but we Bentley owners soon wanted improved performance. A friend fitted a four-and-a-half litre Bentley engine in his three litre model but the chassis was not strong enough. The solution was to shorten the chassis. Forrest Lycett took this to extremes by cutting down an eight litre Bentley into a two-seater capable of 160 mph.

My more practical compromise was a four and a half litre Bentley cut down to just a long bonnet, narrow two-seater cockpit and a 35 gallon petrol tank. In return for completing a form declaring, 'I always use Shell petrol' one qualified for a free fill up at Brooklands. For me this covered the entry fee. Whilst Lycett's car was not practicable for daily use, mine had to be, and was even employed to tow the horse box. I do not believe I was ever overtaken by another vehicle on the open road.

After the war and marriage more sedate cars were required. My first was a 1939 drop-head Railton, which had exceptional acceleration being made of aluminium. Next came a drop-head Sunbeam-Talbot with a hint of art deco in the styling. It was succeeded by a new, very smart Ford drop-head, though with inferior performance, and then by one of the very first minis, thus back to where I had started. I have to admit, however, to a series of Jaguar saloons, theoretically family-friendly, but which found themselves being driven pretty fast.

In retirement, I was able to visit almost any city with a good opera house and a decent art gallery. The furthest I got was San Diego – on the Mexican border of California. I have never been to Australia, but left it to my son Julian to visit Allason Island, a remote paradise on the Great Barrier Reef. My Uncle Harry bought it about 1907 and farmed there successfully. When he died in 1935 he left it to Dr Barnardo's Homes to be used as a boys' camp, but they did not oblige, abandoning it to squatters. With the development of fast launches access became practicable and Barnado's sold it – to the annoyance of the family. It has now become the site of a luxury hotel with more sandy beaches than bedrooms. There are huge flocks of pheasant, descended from those introduced by my uncle, who missed his shooting. The nearest land is too far away for them to fly to, thus they remain the only wild pheasants in Australia.

It is not easy to leave one's name behind. I doubt if the owners of Phuket Airport would be prepared to name it after its originator. Wilberforce is still honoured for the abolition of the slave trade, but I doubt if I shall be remembered as the author of the policy of 'tenants' rights to buy'. So I content myself with the thought that very indirectly I am responsible for the Israelis and Falkland Islanders being free. Mountbatten takes responsibility for the Indonesians.

Appendix 1

The Anglo-Swiss Parliamentary Ski Race

Ernest Marples was an efficiency fanatic, so when he decided to learn to ski he went to the best ski resort, hired the best guide, and devoted three months to the task. After that effort in Davos, he passed his first-class test.

In 1955 Marples was a junior minister in Harold Macmillan's Ministry of Housing, fulfilling the election pledge to build 300,000 houses a year. His Swiss opposite number, hearing that Marples was in Davos, asked for talks, but Marples would accept only if they skied together and held their discussions over lunch. This proved so agreeable that Marples suggested bringing five British MPs to ski for a week with five Swiss, with a race at the end.

Among the earliest Swiss participants were René Bühler, Rudi Suter, Hans Conzett and 'Grendy' Grendelmeyer. The latter was a poor skier and a severe handicap to his team, while Marples was eager to win every time.

René Bühler, with his enthusiasm, charm and generosity, did most to ensure the growth of the meeting from its small beginnings. Bryant Godman Irvine and I, as the successive organisers after Marples, put in a recommendation for an honorary CBE, and when he was awarded this it gave great pleasure to all, especially the Swiss.

One of the very early races was held in a snowstorm, so Aubrey Jones refused to start. His wife took his number and raced instead, revealing her identity at the finish to roars of laughter.

Marples did not seem to realise that it would perhaps be tactful if the Swiss sometimes won in these early days. Although we had triumphed in 1959 and in 1960, he was determined to win again the next year, and led the team to Weissflüh for an early run before the race. At 9 a.m. the snow was hard as rock and I fell, breaking my ankle. The Swiss won narrowly, and the future of the race was assured.

Since the days of Sir Harold Mitchell, who had won the first Inferno race, we have not had an MP who has been in the British ski team. But we have had two wives who have captained the British women's team, Audrey Sale-Barker and Hilary Laing, married respectively to Geordie Selkirk and Boz Ferranti. Their skiing has been inspirational, and I recall an occasion when Hilary challenged her fellow skiers to follow her down a steep slope. When we reached the bottom, I told her, somewhat breathlessly, that I had not skied so fast for years; looking back for our companions, we saw them scattered across the slope, recumbent.

In the first twenty years, numbers grew from five a side to about twenty, and the Swiss became dominant. The first assistance offered was to allow the British captain to choose the number of competitors to count. In 1972 I chose six, and half our team turned out to live in my constituency, being Cecil Parkinson, myself and John Sandford, then a curate in Harpenden, and a hereditary peer. His full title, the Right Honourable Lieutenant-Commander the Reverend Lord Sandford, was a bit of a mouthful even for those used to coping with the complexities of the peerage.

In 1973 I chose seven a side and had I chosen eight, we would have won, a feat never repeated without a time handicap. That was the year John Cordle came out, but said he could not race as he was only a beginner. I told him that if he was accepting lavish Swiss hospitality, he must at least start. He defeated me by turning up supported by two guides, one each side, who eased him down the course. His photograph was published worldwide as the way British MPs skied.

A prize-giving dinner, usually held at Wolfgang, was hosted alternately by each side. Of course, finance was a difficulty when it was the British turn, while exchange controls were strictly enforced, and I cannot remember all the ingenious stratagems we used. But having Jack Diamond as a competitor was a help while he was Chief Secretary to the Treasury in Harold Wilson's Cabinet. During a blizzard at Weissflüh he said to me, 'My colleagues think this is the sport of the idle rich.'

When there were only about twelve a side, we were able to give souvenirs to the whole team, frequently the very decorative House of Commons ashtrays. In the year the Churchill souvenir crowns were minted, however, I was giving some out to the Swiss competitors when Harold Spence's tactless wife Beryl, remarked in an audible voice from the back of the room, 'They're only worth five bob.'

When our French Parliamentary counterparts got to hear of the race they asked to send an observer, followed by a request to join in, which was declined by the Swiss. This was the origin of the annual European Parliamentary Ski Championship, with teams from Germany and Italy as well as France. The Swiss would not send a team, but Fred Rubi, the ex-Olympic skier, could not resist turning up to win the individual cup. This competition did not last long, and in the absence of the Swiss, was always won by the British.

The Prince of Wales competed only once, and at the other end of the scale, Philip Goodhart has missed few races since his first, in 1959. Famously, in January 1981, the Goodharts received a telephone call at the Fluella from London, and a woman's voice asked to speak to Philip. Val said, 'I'm afraid you can't because he's in the bath.' The reply was, 'Will you tell him this is the Prime Minister speaking.' Philip was out of the bath in a flash and was appointed Army Minister. He offered to return to London at once, but Mrs Thatcher told him to stay and compete in the race.

Ian Orr-Ewing, another fine skier, was there from the start and for many years was one of our best competitors. As he grew old, he refused to make any concessions to himself, but, brave as a lion, insisted on skiing with the top group. Finally, in his eighties, he fell most of the way down an icy Meierhof glade, and Joanie insisted that he retire. He was never involved in the organisation of the meeting, which lay on the British side with the officers of the British–Swiss Parliamentary Group, but he was loud in his criticisms, which did not always go down well with the Swiss. His ashes now lie on the Parsenn.

Sir John Hunt, who led the first successful expedition to climb Everest, came once or twice. He did not appreciate a newspaper report that he was faster uphill than down, and having to endure the complaints of Lady Hunt, a strict socialist of the old school, about our apparently prodigious consumption of luxury.

One of the adept consumers was Charles Taylor, always our best-dressed competitor, dazzling in his bright yellow skin-tight trousers. Not everyone followed his sartorial example, and Pat Limerick, a distinguished mountaineer, considered his oldest clothes suitable for the mountains, and always carried a huge rucksack. On one occasion, when we were skiing down the south face of the Weissflüh-gipfel, two of our party managed to fall down a twenty-foot vertical face. Pat instantly reached into his backpack and had a rope down to them to complete the rescue.

I also carried a small bag of essentials, such as a pendulum to tell you which way up you were when engulfed in an avalanche, and a metallic space blanket in which Toby Jessell was once wrapped on one of his several trips in the blood-wagon down to the Krankenhaus.

Paddy Ashdown was never without his rucksack, as if to remind the world how tough he was. He even carried it in the race. One year, one of our MPs (not, on this occasion, Paddy) put the daughter of a Swiss MP in the family way. The next year Toby Jessell was surprised to have his face slapped by the new grandmother, who mistook him for the seducer.

My son, Rupert Allason, started to compete in the sons' race in 1965, and continued until he qualified for the main race in 1988 as an MP. I had the idea of presenting a prize for the best two close relatives competing but then realised that we would be hopelessly beaten by Eddie Digby and his nephew Winston Churchill.

The Osborn Cup for Veterans was, I thought, intended for long-time competitors who reached their seventies. When I won it at the age of seventy-nine, I had competed for much of the previous thirty-two years. Now it seems to be won by elderly but very fit Swiss, turning up for the first time.

Ernest Marples came as a spectator to one of our races in the 1990s. When he and Lady Marples arrived late at the dinner at the Fluella there was no place for them at the top table. The founder of the race had been forgotten.

Appendix 2

'Euro Deficits' from *Britain*, Spring 2003

When a country runs into irreversible economic difficulties, it can escape by devaluing the currency. Everyone receives a lower income in world terms, but it is not immediately noticeable. 'The pound in your pocket has not been devalued,' as Harold Wilson claimed. Imports, including raw materials, become more expensive, but exports and tourism are encouraged.

The remedy is not open to a country in the Eurozone that runs into difficulties. Its government expenditure, including social security, is paid in Euros, and is very difficult to reduce. Borrowing only postpones the evil day, if a lender can be found. Most banks have already burnt their fingers on optimistic loans to unreliable risks. Such a government must increase taxation, encouraging mobile labour, the wealthy and industry to move elsewhere. This reduces the tax base, requiring still further taxation.

An alternative for a country in difficulties is to leave the Euro, either by application or expulsion. The country would return to its old currency at the rate that it joined the Euro, and then immediately devalue.

After devaluation, the country would be unable to return to the Euro at the new rate, since those receiving money from the government, such as government servants and pensioners, would receive fewer Euros, and see the con.

A solution, especially if several countries were economically involved, would appear to be to centralise Eurozone budgets in the EU, with unified tax rates. There would be exemptions of tax for those on low incomes, of course. Small farmers can enjoy a satisfactory way of life by principally using barter, so very little revenue could be expected from agricultural areas.

The EU would, however, have to provide for the whole Eurozone infrastructure, plus the cost of pensions for those countries that have failed to fund their pensions. The mind boggles in contemplation of the level of taxation that would need to be imposed on the inhabitants of cities and industrial areas, plus those of the wealthy who have not left.

The EU is not celebrated for its ability to combat fraud. The ultimate solution will be to abolish the Euro and return to the market.

Acknowledgements

My contribution to this book is entirely based on memory, recollections that remain very much alive. The research was carried out by my two sons and my cousin Harry Stone, all, themselves, authors. I thank them for their hard work and encouragement.

I am entirely grateful to Heather Wooster, who for several years has deciphered my cryptic handwriting over a series of drafts. I also owe a debt of gratitude to Lady Celestria Hales for reviewing the draft, and to Mandy Lampard for her creative help with the cover and pictures.

My thanks are also due to the Imperial War Museum and other copyright holders who so kindly gave their consent to the reproduction of photographs. Also to my grandson, Jamie Allason, for taking the picture of Chacombe Priory: it brings back many happy memories.

Acronyms

ADC	Aide de Camp
BAOR	British Army of the Rhine
CIA	Central Intelligence Agency
CIGS	Chief of the Imperial General Staff
ECO	Emergency Commissioned Officer
GSO1	General Staff Officer Grade 1
HCYC	House of Commons Yacht Club
MI5	Security Service
ORQMS	Orderly Room Quartermaster Sergeant
PPS	Parliamentary Private Secretary
SAS	22nd Special Air Service Regiment
SEAC	South East Asia Command
SIB	Army Special Investigation Branch
SIS	Secret Intelligence Service
TCPA	Town and Country Planning Association

Index